Dewey Decimal Classification
Edition 21 and International Perspectives

Dewey Decimal Classification
Edition 21 and International Perspectives

Papers from a Workshop
Presented at the General Conference
of the International Federation of
Library Associations and Institutions (IFLA)
Beijing, China
August 29, 1996

Edited by Lois Mai Chan and Joan S. Mitchell

Sponsored by the IFLA Section
on Classification and Indexing
and
OCLC Forest Press

FOREST PRESS
A Division of
OCLC Online Computer Library Center, Inc.
Albany, New York
1997

Library of Congress Cataloging-in-Publication Data

Dewey decimal classification : edition 21 and international perspectives : papers from a workshop presented at the General Conference of the International Federation of Library Associations and Institutions (IFLA), August 29, 1996 / edited by Lois Mai Chan and Joan S. Mitchell.
    p.   cm.
    "Sponsored by the Section on Classification and Indexing, IFLA and OCLC Forest Press."
    ISBN 0-910608-56-3 (alk. paper)
    1. Classification, Dewey decimal--Congresses.   I. Chan, Lois Mai. II. Mitchell, Joan S. III. International Federation of Library Associations and Institutions. Section on Classification and Indexing. IV. Forest Press. V. IFLA General Conference (1996)
Z696.D7D49   1996
025.4'31--DC21

                          96-48761
                              CIP

Contents

Foreword
    Donna Duncan   **vii**

Dewey Decimal Classification:
Edition 21 and International Perspectives   **1**
OPENING REMARKS
    Lois Mai Chan

DDC 21: An Introduction   **3**
    Joan S. Mitchell

The Revision of 350–354 Public Administration and
560–590 Life Sciences in Edition 21 of the DDC   **17**
    Giles S. Martin

Dewey for Windows   **29**
    Julianne Beall

The Dewey Decimal Classification System in
National Bibliographies   **43**
    Barbara L. Bell

The DDC in the Asia-Pacific Region   **59**
    Giles S. Martin

The Dewey Decimal Classification in China   **67**
    Wang Dongbo

Translating the DDC: The Experience of
the Spanish Version   **77**
    Octavio G. Rojas L.

Dewey Decimal Classification: Organizing
the World of Knowledge for the World   **85**
SUMMARY AND CLOSING REMARKS
    Lois Mai Chan

Contributors   **97**

Foreword

On behalf of the IFLA Section on Classification and Indexing, I would like to welcome you to the workshop on *Dewey Decimal Classification: Edition 21 and International Perspectives*, cosponsored by the Section and OCLC Forest Press. This workshop will provide a forum for teachers, practitioners, and advocates of the Dewey Decimal Classification.

The aims of the workshop are to introduce, present revisions and expansions, and clarify the twenty-first edition of the Dewey Decimal Classification in both print and electronic versions. The international use of the DDC, the use of the DDC in national bibliographies, and the translation of the DDC will also be presented and discussed.

I would like to thank OCLC Forest Press, especially Joan Mitchell, Editor, Dewey Decimal Classification, and Julianne Beall, Assistant Editor, Dewey Decimal Classification, for their support and efforts in making this workshop possible. Also, kudos to the speakers for their informative and thought-provoking papers.

Thank you for choosing this workshop. May you have a profitable, enjoyable, and memorable day.

Donna Duncan
Chairperson, IFLA Section
on Classification and Indexing

Dewey Decimal Classification
Edition 21 and International Perspectives

OPENING REMARKS

Lois Mai Chan

In the past two decades, we have seen the most spectacular changes and advances in the formation, access, and delivery of information. The impact of such changes equals, if not surpasses, the industrial revolution. We are living in an era aptly called the "information age." The dramatic changes in information transfer that we are experiencing bear not only on the nature of the information itself but also on its volume; for the latter, the amount of information that passes through the Internet every day, in fact every minute or second, is indeed mind-boggling.

In this "big bang" of exploding information, where the units of the information universe are more diverse and fragmented in nature and origin than has been the case for formally published material, information and computer professionals are searching for efficient and effective ways to organize and deliver the amount and kinds of information that are now available. One method currently being investigated on many fronts is the use of classification schemes, including those that have been used for years, to organize large amounts of information in libraries. Among these is the Dewey Decimal Classification (DDC).

In 1876, a college librarian developed a novel scheme for organizing his library's collection; this was Melvil Dewey, the man for whom the DDC is named. Over the past 120 years, the original scheme has grown to become the most widely used library classification system in the world. During those years, through revisions and expansions, the scheme has adapted to continuing changes in the nature and volume of information units. Nevertheless, certain fundamental features of the DDC have remained: these include, first, the principle of hierarchy in both its structure and its decimal notation; second, its suitability for use at different levels of information organization; and, third, its adaptability to different cultural environments.

The scheme, now in its twenty-first edition which was published this summer, can truly be considered an international standard. It has been translated into over thirty languages, and has been adopted by libraries around the world. Its widespread use and in particular its numerical notation make it an important factor in furthering the international exchange of information. And the wide availability of DDC classification data enhances international bibliographic control.

In today's workshop, we invite you to examine how the scheme has attempted, with varying degrees of success, to meet different demands in different parts of the world. In the morning session, planned particularly for those who have been Dewey users, the speakers will not only outline and discuss the major changes in Edition 21, but will also describe other new developments relating to the use of the system. In the afternoon, our speakers' main focus will be on matters relating to use of the DDC in the international sphere.

DDC 21: An Introduction
Joan S. Mitchell

INTRODUCTION

In this paper, I will present a general introduction to Edition 21, the new edition of the Dewey Decimal Classification.[1] I will also briefly describe the underlying database and some new uses of Dewey in the electronic information environment.

The twenty-first edition of the Dewey Decimal Classification has just been published in print and electronic versions. Edition 21 contains changes in the organization of several disciplines. It also provides expansions for new areas of knowledge, accommodates many political and social changes, and includes updated terminology. Edition 21 also features several structural changes that make the Classification easier to apply, reflect modern classification design principles, and support electronic distribution.

MAJOR REVISIONS

Schedules are revised to reflect new views of the field, to provide for new topics, and to correct existing problems in bias and structure. Edition 21 includes three major revisions: 350–354 Public administration, 370 Education, and 560–590 Life sciences. The changes in public administration and education have been underway for more than a decade; the changes in the life sciences for more than two. In addition to review and approval by the Decimal Classification Editorial Policy Committee, each revision has been reviewed by committees appointed by the American Library Association (ALA) and the Library Association in the U.K.

PUBLIC ADMINISTRATION

Public administration is completely revised. The schedule still occupies 351–354, but the subdivisions and citation order have been changed. The revision addresses several longstanding problems in the discipline:

1. The basic structure of the 350s was a problem—it forced the classifier to make illogical distinctions among central governments (351), specific central governments (353–354), and comprehensive works on central and local governments (350);

3

2. The schedule gave preference to jurisdiction first, even though interest in the field of public administration has been focused more on topic;

3. The schedule displayed U.S. bias in structure and terminology.

In the new public administration schedule, the structure is improved, the U.S. bias is reduced, and the citation order is reversed from jurisdiction/topic to topic/jurisdiction. The last reflects the shift in the literature of the discipline away from jurisdiction to topic as the central emphasis. The schedule also makes use of facet indicators and notational synthesis to represent recurring topics. Here is an example that illustrates some of the changes:

Administration of natural resources by U.S. state governments
Ed. 20: 353.938232
353.93 Base number for Administration of specific fields [in U.S. State governments]
8232 Natural resources and their conservation (from 351.8232)

Ed. 21: 354.32130973
354.3 Base number for Administration of environment and natural resources
2 Facet indicator for General considerations (internal table under 352–354)
13 State and provincial administration (from 352.13)
09 Facet indicator for Geographic treatment (Table 1 notation as instructed in internal table under 352.13–352.19)
73 United States (Table 2)

The following example shows the changes in the Classification for the same topic (administration of natural resources) by a similar jurisdictional level (provincial government) in Canada:

Administration of natural resources by Canadian provincial governments
Ed. 20: 354.71008232
354 Base number for Administration of specific central governments
71 Canada (Table 2)
00 Facet indicator for Administration of specific fields (internal table under 354.3–.9)
8232 Natural resources and their conservation (from 351.8232)

Ed. 21: 354.32130971

354.3 Base number for Administration of environment and natural resources

2 Facet indicator for General considerations (internal table under 352–354)

13 State and provincial administration (from 352.13)

09 Facet indicator for Geographic treatment (Table 1 notation as instructed in internal table under 352.13–352.19)

71 Canada (Table 2)

Notice in Edition 21 that the numbers for the U.S. and Canadian examples differ only in the final two digits—the notation for the specific area. Thus works on the same topic in different jurisdictions are now collocated in Edition 21.

EDUCATION

370 Education represents an extensive revision. This means that the main outline of the schedule has remained the same, but some subdivisions have been reworked and expansions provided for new topics.

The most visible changes are the relocation of 376 Education of women and 377 Schools and religion to subdivisions of 371. The revised schedule reflects the current view in the discipline of education that each of these topics is an aspect of a broader topic (i.e., kind of student and type of school, respectively) rather than a central division of education. For example:

371.82 Specific kinds of students; schools for specific kinds of students
Add to base number 371.82 the numbers following —08 in notation 081–089 from Table 1, e.g., education of women 371.822 [*formerly* 376], education of students by racial, ethnic, national origin 371.829 . . .

In Edition 21, the number for the education of women (371.822) shares the same base number (371.82) as the education of other kinds of persons, e.g., girls 371.823, Chinese students 371.829951, Asian Americans 371.82995073.

Religious schools have moved from class 377 to within class 371 as an aspect of types of schools:

> 371.01–371.07   Specific kinds of schools

371.07   Religious schools

371.071   Christian religious schools
Add to base number 371.071 the numbers
following 28 in 281–289, e.g., Catholic schools
371.0712

371.072 –.079   Other religious schools
Add to base number 371.07 the numbers
following 29 in 292–299, e.g., Islamic
schools 371.077

The notation used to describe the specific kind of religious school
comes from the 200 Religion schedule:

Catholic schools	371.071<u>2</u> (from 28<u>2</u>)
Russian Orthodox schools	371.071<u>1947</u> (from 281<u>.9</u> + —<u>47</u> from Table 2)
Jewish day schools	371.07<u>6</u> (from 29<u>6</u>)
Islamic schools	371.07<u>7</u> (from 29<u>7</u>)

The new education schedule is accompanied by a development of —07,
the notation in Table 1 for education, research, related topics:

—07	Education, research, related topics
—071	Education (former heading: Schools and courses)
—072	Research; statistical methods
—0727	Statistical methods
—0728	Presentation of statistical data
—0785	Computer-assisted instruction

We have regularized the use of —07 at 370.7, which means that we
have replaced the special development for standard subdivision concepts at that number with regular use of notation 07 from Table 1. The
biggest relocation is the move of educational research from 370.78 to
regular use of 370.72.

There are a few other changes to mention in education. Sociology
of education has moved out of 370 Education to join the sociology of
other disciplines in 306. Home schools have been relocated from
the 640s to a specific number (371.042) under alternative schools.
There is an expansion for elementary reading and language arts and
provision for distance education. The index includes many new terms
in education, such as school choice, textbook bias, critical peda-
gogy, and whole language approach.

LIFE SCIENCES

The third major revision, 560–590 Life sciences, has been underway for over two decades. This revision combines the two approaches to revision displayed in public administration and education.[2] Like public administration, the 570 schedule is completely revised, along with 583 Dicotyledons. Like education, the rest of 560–590 is extensively revised. Again, this means that the main outline of the rest of 560–590 has remained basically the same.

The new 570 schedule features a reversal in citation order from organism/process to process/organism that in turn addresses a fundamental shift in the discipline away from a focus on organism to a focus on internal biological process. The new schedule collocates microorganisms, fungi, and algae in 579; uses notation 1 to introduce general topics throughout the taxonomic schedules 579–590; provides more specific and shorter numbers for fishes and mammals; and makes regular use of facet indicators and notational synthesis.

In the new arrangement of 570, we have left 574 vacant, as well as the first third of 575. When we studied the distribution of materials in the old number in the OCLC database, we found that 80 percent of materials in the 570s were classed in 574 and the first part of 575. By leaving all of 574 and 575–575.3 vacant, we hope to minimize the impact on libraries of adopting the new schedule.

Here is an example that illustrates some of the changes in the life sciences:

Metabolism in bears
Ed. 20:   599.7444604133
599.74446   Bears
04   Facet indicator for Processes and parts (internal table under 592–599)
1   Physiology (from 591.1 Physiology of animals)
33   Metabolism (from 574.133)

Ed. 21:   572.41978
572.4   Metabolism
1   Facet indicator for specific animal (from 571.1 Animals)
978   Bears (from 599.78 Bears)

Notice that the number for bears is much shorter—one of the goals was to provide shorter and more specific numbers for mammals. The changes in the numbers for some animals have a ripple effect throughout the Classification where 590 notation is used to build numbers: 333.95 Biological resources; 636.9 [Animal husbandry of] Other mammals; 639 Hunting, fishing, conservation, related technologies; 799.1 Fishing; and 799.2 Hunting.

RELIGION

In addition to the three major revisions of disciplines described above, there have been numerous other changes to address cultural, social, and political issues. With Edition 21, we have initiated a multi-edition plan to further reduce Christian bias in 200 Religion. We have moved comprehensive works on Christianity from 200 to 230, and have relocated the standard subdivisions of Christianity from 201–209 to 230–270. The standard subdivisions of comparative religion are now integrated with the standard subdivisions of religion in 200.1–200.9. We have revised and expanded the schedules for two major religions, 296 Judaism and 297 Islam, and have provided optional arrangements for books of Tanakh, the Jewish Bible. The revisions of Judaism and Islam have been reviewed by committees appointed by ALA and the Library Association in the U.K. The revision and expansion of Islam was also reviewed by the Cataloging Committee of the Africana Librarians Council in the African Studies Association.

COMPUTER SCIENCE

Another area of change is 004–006 Computer science. The computer science schedule was published as a separate in 1985, and incorporated into Edition 20 in 1989. Even though the schedule is relatively new, the field has changed so rapidly in the last ten years that we have had to update and expand it. In Edition 20, computer science was organized and/or subdivided by type of computer. In Edition 21, that organization/subdivision has been extended to include operating system, user interface, and processing mode. There are also provisions for new topics such as graphical user interfaces, Internet, and connectionism.

OTHER CHANGES

Here are some highlights of selected other changes in the schedules and Tables 1 and 3. In 340 Law, we have moved the main instructions from 340 to 342–349, and have modified the headings of the main spans 342–349 and 342–347 to reflect the content of their component classes. With its adoption of Edition 21, the Library of Congress will no longer assign Option B in 340 Law.

We have revised and expanded 368 Insurance. In the 390s, specific holidays have been relocated from 394.268 to 394.261–394.267 to provide a better arrangement and shorter numbers. Tales and lore by place have been relocated from 398.21–398.27 to 398.2093–398.2099. The new span includes an internal add table for topics. Both changes in the 390s were announced prior to publication in Edition 21 in issues of *Dewey Decimal Classification, Additions, Notes and Decisions (DC&)*. At 940–990, we have introduced a new add table for recurring topics related to wars, e.g., land, air, naval operations.

In my discussion of the revision of 370 Education, I described the changes in Table 1 notation 07. Other changes in Table 1 include new numbers for apparatus, equipment, materials (—0284); waste technology (—0286); boys six to eleven (—08341); girls six to eleven (—08342); collected persons treatment of members of specific racial, ethnic, national groups (—0923); and biographies of animals (part of persons treatment of nonhumans [—0929]). Table 1 now uses the general meaning of "young adults" (persons in early adulthood) as opposed to the library-specific usage of the term for adolescents. Comprehensive works on young adults have been moved from —0835 to —0842.

Table 3-C notation 1 (Arts and literature displaying specific qualities of style, mood, viewpoint) and notation 3 (Arts and literature dealing with specific themes and subjects) have been expanded and approved for use with 700.4, a new number for special topics in the arts. For example:

Surrealism in the arts
Ed. 21: 700.41163
700.41   Arts displaying specific qualities of style, mood, viewpoint
163   Number following —1 in notation 1163 Surrealism (Table 3-C)

AREAS, PERIODS, PEOPLES, LANGUAGES

There are numerous adjustments in Edition 21 to reflect political changes, such as the major revision of the area table for the countries of the former Soviet Union. We have worked with national libraries and other groups to prepare revisions of the area tables for Brazil, Colombia, Greece, New Zealand, Nigeria, and Norway.

We have added a new historical period in South Africa for the administration of Nelson Mandela and a new literary period for South Africa starting in 1994. Even though we have just issued Edition 21, we are already working on a revision of the South Africa area table to reflect recent changes in the political divisions of the country.

We have provided several expansions for languages in Table 6 (e.g., African languages, North and South American native languages, Polynesian languages), and for peoples in Table 5 (e.g., Kurds, Balachi, Miao [Hmong]).

NEW TOPICS AND REVISED TERMINOLOGY

Many new topics that have gained literary warrant since the publication of Edition 20 are now mentioned explicitly in Edition 21. Among these topics are bungee jumping, family leave, in-line skating, Internet, mountain biking, neural nets, rap music, snowboarding, and virtual reality.

Terminology throughout the Classification has been updated to achieve currency, ensure sensitivity, and reflect international usage. Many of the changes in terminology have resulted from a concerted effort to provide descriptive representations in the schedules of persons, social groups, national groups, etc., using the terminology preferred by the group and understood by an international audience. Here are some examples of old and new descriptions from the schedules:

Gypsies	>>	Romany people
Handicapped	>>	Persons with disabilities
Lapps	>>	Sami
Old persons	>>	Older persons

Since the Classification is used by 200,000 libraries in 135 countries, we have also introduced several features to meet international or special needs. We have extended the entry vocabulary in the Relative Index to include terminology in use outside of the United States in countries using the English-language standard edition. Some examples include GCSE (educational tests in the U.K.) and CEGEP (a type of educational institution in Canada). The grade-level equivalents for the specific levels of education found in 372.24 and 373.23 are explained in a Manual note to assist users in countries with other patterns of educational levels. We have also added options to address special needs, such as the optional arrangement for books of Tanakh found in the Manual note for 221 and at 296.11 in the schedule.

STRUCTURAL CHANGES

Edition 21 also includes several structural changes. These changes include simplification of the notes structure, improvement of captions, regularization, increased use of facet indicators and notational synthesis, and expansion of the Manual and Relative Index.

The note structure in the schedules has been simplified by combining example, contains, and including notes into a single note type, the "including" note. In addition, "standard-subdivisions-are-added" notes have been introduced in many entries with multiterm captions to make clear which topics approximate the whole of the concept represented by the number. For example:

378.12   Faculty and teaching
                 Standard subdivisions are added for faculty
              and teaching together, for faculty alone

Standard subdivisions are not added for teaching alone because that topic has its own number further down the hierarchy in 378.125.

In Edition 21, we have reduced adjectival headings, prepositional phrases, and many vague headings. Within the print edition, it is relatively easy to glance at the page header or up the hierarchy on a page to put a heading in context. When schedules are used in an electronic environment, the individual records have no context unless viewed in separate page displays or hierarchical displays. Fuller captions assist the classifier and may help the end user as the Classification (beyond the notation itself) is used in new applications, e.g., to organize World Wide Web resources. I will return to this topic at the end of my paper.

In recent editions, we have made a conscious move away from enumeration in the schedules. Where possible without substantial disruption to existing collections, we have replaced special developments for standard subdivision concepts with use of regular standard subdivisions found in Table 1. We call this process *regularization.*

For example, I mentioned earlier that the development at 370.7 Education, research, related topics now matches the development of notation 07 in Table 1. The geographic distribution of temperature at the earth's surface has been moved from a special development at 551.5252 to regular use of Table 1 geographic notation 09 at 551.525.

The new public administration schedule and the life sciences schedule share one common feature beyond revision: both make extensive use of facet indicators and notational synthesis. Why are facet indicators and notational synthesis important? The use of facet indicators to identify meaningful components in a number and the use of uniform notation to express recurring aspects of topics make the Classification easier to apply and offer potential in retrieval. Let us return to our bear example for a minute.

The facet indicator 1 links the topic "metabolism" to its treatment in a specific animal. The use of standard notation for bears provides a hierarchical link to broader concepts (land carnivores 599.7, mammals 599) and to narrower concepts (grizzly/brown bears 599.784, American black bear 599.785). By using standard notation to represent bears throughout the Classification, we are able to retrieve topics related to bears (mammals), and not retrieve topics related to teddy bears (toys). For example:

Bears	599.<u>78</u>
animal husbandry	636.9<u>78</u>
big game hunting	799.27<u>78</u>
conservation technology	639.979<u>78</u>
resource economics	333.959<u>78</u>

Several years ago, Songqiao Liu demonstrated the feasibility of algorithmically "decomposing" Dewey numbers into their component parts.[3] Research remains to be done to explore the use of Dewey facets in browsing and information retrieval.

Another structural change in Edition 21 is the expansion of the Manual and Relative Index. The Manual is almost one hundred pages longer. Every major revision has an introductory note. The notes in public administration and the life sciences include sample titles illustrating the changes in the major revisions. There are also notes with sample titles for other areas, such as music, computer science, language, and literature. The Manual is also now indexed in the Relative Index. Here is an example:

Meteorology	551.5
	T1—015 515
aeronautics	629.132 4
agriculture	630.251 5
see Manual at 551.5 vs. 551.6	

The last line, "*see Manual at* 551.5 vs. 551.6," means that "Meteorology" is one of the index terms for the Manual note at 551.5 vs. 551.6.

In addition to the new entries for Manual notes, the Relative Index contains more terms, including entries for selected built numbers and terms to provide entry vocabulary for international users. The electronic version of the Relative Index includes more terms than can be accommodated in the print version. For example, in the print Relative Index, the concepts of wetland biology and wetland ecology are indexed under "Wetlands" with the subheadings of "biology" and "ecology." The electronic Relative Index includes the same entries as the print version plus the phrases "wetland biology" and "wetland ecology." These electronic terms can be accessed through Dewey for Windows, the Microsoft Windows™-based CD-ROM version of Edition 21.[4]

THE DDC DATABASE

Many of the structural changes in the Classification are motivated by present and future uses of the underlying database. The database is maintained and updated using the Editorial Support System (ESS), a UNIX-based system with DDC-specific fields. Before work began on Edition 21, several ESS fields were modified or added to accommodate elements in the USMARC Format for Classification Data.[5] One of the new fields in Edition 21 is the 685 history note field. We have used the 685 field to document the history of many expanded, relocated, and discontinued numbers from Editions 19 to 20, and Editions 20 to 21. This information resides in the ESS database, and could be employed in online systems to guide users to relevant information split between former and current numbers.

Another change in the underlying database is the incorporation of selected Library of Congress subject headings. Library of Congress subject headings have always been a source for terminology in the Relative Index, but their inclusion depends upon literary warrant for the concept and compatibility with the rules for Relative Index entries. Electronic Dewey, the DOS-based version of Edition 20, contained statistically mapped Library of Congress subject headings derived from the OCLC Online Union Catalog (OLUC).[6] Dewey for Windows also includes statistically mapped LC subject headings. However, because the OLUC did not have any examples of records classified under the major revisions when we were preparing the Edition 21 database, we have supplemented the statistical mappings with selected LC subject headings mapped by the editors. We plan to continue mapping selected new LC subject headings to candidate Edition 21 numbers. This will permit the faster linking of new topics to the Classification, and will provide classifiers with advice as to where such topics should be classed.

We will use our Dewey home page (http://www.oclc.org/fp/) as a vehicle for this information. Some of these mappings may be incorporated into future versions of the database.

BEYOND EDITON 21

The DDC database today serves as the basis for standard English-language print and electronic editions, translations, and various research projects. Some exciting research projects are underway to use the Classification in new ways. Diane Vizine-Goetz is experimenting with revised DDC summaries to serve as a browser for NetFirst™, an OCLC database of Internet resources.[7] Pauline Cochrane and Eric Johnson are using the database to explore the development of an end-user browsing mechanism using amplified DDC captions without DDC numbers.[8]

Another research effort is focusing on use of recent translations to develop a multilingual browser. Over the years, the DDC has been translated into over thirty languages. Recent translations in progress or completed include Arabic, Chinese, French, Greek, Hebrew, Italian, Persian, Russian, Spanish, and Turkish. OCLC Research is developing a multilingual browser based on the summaries of several recent translations with the Dewey notation as the common language.[9] A prototype is available on the Dewey home page.

These research projects will enable libraries to extend their shelves into the global environment. Each also has the potential to help us improve the Classification for all users.

NOTES

1. Melvil Dewey, *Dewey Decimal Classification and Relative Index*, 21st ed., ed. Joan S. Mitchell, Julianne Beall, Winton E. Matthews, Jr., and Gregory R. New, 4 vols. (Albany, N.Y.: OCLC Forest Press, 1996).

2. For a discussion of the reasons behind the different approaches to revision, see Gregory R. New, "Revision and Stability in Dewey 21: The Life Sciences Catch Up," in *Knowledge Organization and Change: Proceedings of the 4th International ISKO Conference, 15–18 July 1996, Washington, D.C.*, ed. Rebecca Green (Frankfurt/Main: INDEKS Verlag, 1996), 386–95.

3. Songqiao Liu, "The Automatic Decomposition of DDC Synthesized Numbers" (Ph.D. diss., University of California, Los Angeles, 1993).

4. Dewey for Windows, Version 1.00, OCLC Forest Press, Dublin, Ohio.

5. Julianne Beall, "Editing the Dewey Decimal Classification Online: The Evolution of the DDC Database," in *Classification Research for Knowledge Representation and Organization: Proceedings of the 5th International Study Conference on Classification Research, Toronto, Canada, June 24–28, 1991*, ed. Nancy J. Williamson and Michèle Hudon (Amsterdam and New York: Elsevier, 1992), 29–37.

6. Electronic Dewey, Version 1.01, OCLC Forest Press, Dublin, Ohio.

7. Diane Vizine-Goetz, "Online Classification: Implications for Classifying and Document[-like] Object Retrieval," in *Knowledge Organization and Change*, 249–53.

8. Pauline Cochrane and Eric Johnson, "Visual Dewey: DDC in a Hypertextual Browser for the Library User," in *Knowledge Organization and Change*, 95–105.

9. Diane Vizine-Goetz, and Joan S. Mitchell, "Dewey 2000," in *Annual Review of OCLC Research 1995* (Dublin, Ohio: OCLC, 1996), 16–19.

The Revision of 350–354 Public Administration and 560–590 Life Sciences in Edition 21 of the DDC

Giles S. Martin

INTRODUCTION

The Dewey Decimal Classification is caught between two schools of thought:

- Those who think that classification numbers should never change, and that you should accommodate new subjects in the spaces between old numbers; and

- Those who think that the whole scheme should be recast, to provide a more logical foundation, based on current knowledge, and to avoid cultural biases.

The editors of the Classification and the Decimal Classification Editorial Policy Committee (EPC) try to steer a middle course between the two schools of thought. Thus they partially satisfy both, but fully satisfy neither. In particular, with each edition, there are what used to be called "phoenix schedules," and are now called "complete revisions."

Over the last thirty or so years, the major phoenix schedules or complete revisions have included:

Edition 17 (1965)
    150 Psychology
Edition 18 (1971)
    340 Law
    510 Mathematics
Edition 19 (1979)
    301–307 Sociology
Edition 20 (1989)
    004–006 Data processing   Computer science
    780 Music
Edition 21 (1996)
    350–354 Public administration
    570 Biology
    583 Magnoliopsida (Dicotyledons)

The complete revisions of 570 and 583 in Edition 21 form an integral part of a revision of 560–590 Life sciences. Thus a larger part of the schedules is revised in Edition 21 than in any other recent edition.

The revisions of 350–354 Public administration and of 560–590 Life sciences go back a long time before my involvement with EPC— in the case of 560–590, back more than twenty years, to the early 1970s.

350–354 PUBLIC ADMINISTRATION

Problems with the old scheme

The arrangement of 350–354 in Edition 20 and in previous editions had at least three problems:

1. Illogical arrangement. In particular, the first level of classification distinguished between:

350 Public administration (in general)
351 Administration of central governments
352 Administration of local governments
353 Administration of United States federal and state
    governments
354 Administration of specific central governments;
    international administration

This arrangement broke the normal DDC pattern of classifying by topic within a discipline. In 353–354 you first classed by jurisdiction, then by specific fields of public administration (i.e., topic). Furthermore, the distinction made between 350 and 351 is not a distinction found in the literature of public administration.

2. Difficult number building. The instructions in 354 for building numbers for specific fields of administration in specific jurisdictions were difficult to use and often led to over-long numbers.

3. United States bias. The whole of 353 was given to public administration in the United States, and the rest of the world shared 354: this was an allocation of numbers that might have suited libraries in the United States, but which made life more difficult for the rest of us.

The scheme in Edition 21

The main features of the revision of 350–354 Public administration in Edition 21 are:

- Subdivision first by topic, and then by jurisdiction. This reverses the usual pattern in Edition 20 of division first by jurisdiction, and then by topic; and

- Faceting. Edition 21 continues the trend found in the revision of 780 Music, by providing a notation in which several different facets of a topic can be combined in one classification number.

The overall structure of 350–354 Public administration in Edition 21 is:

> 350 *Public administration and military science*
> 351 *Public administration*
> 352–354 *Specific topics of public administration*
>   352 *General considerations of public administration*
>   353 *Specific fields of public administration*
>   354 *Public administration of economy and environment*

Where to start in classifying public administration

Public administration overlaps with other disciplines. For example, 353.6 (Public administration of health services) overlaps with 344.04 (Public health law), with 362.1 (Problems of and services to persons with physical illness), and with 362.1068 (Management of those services). There are Manual notes at T1—068 vs. 353–354; at 300, 320.6 vs. 352–354; at 320.9, 320.4 vs. 351; and at 350 vs. 342–347—these all deal with aspects of this question.

One fundamental distinction is that "public administration" refers primarily to running government agencies that regulate and exercise control of various fields, while "management" refers to running organizations, public or private, that directly perform the work within their scope (Manual T1—068 vs. 353–354).

In general, in cases of doubt, the order of preference is:

1. Numbers outside 340 and 350
2. 350
3. 340

Faceting in 350–354

The different aspects of public administration provided for are divided into:

- Fields of activity (i.e., topics in 353–354);

- General considerations (i.e. topics in 352, such as jurisdictional levels, financial administration, and personnel administration); and

- Standard subdivisions (including geographic treatment).

For complex topics (i.e., topics involving more than one of these aspects), the order of preference is last topic in the schedule, as instructed at 352–354. You can add topics from 352 by using facet 2, and then standard subdivisions in the usual way. For example:

352.14 Local administration
352.140994 Local administration in Australia (352.14 + 0994)

352.67 Conditions of employment
352.670994 Conditions of employment in the Australian public services (352.67 + 0994)
352.67214 Conditions of employment in local government (352.67 + 214)
352.672140994 Conditions of employment in local government in Australia (352.67 + 214 + 0994)

354.335 Prevention and control of pollution
354.3350994 Prevention and control of pollution in Australia (354.335 + 0994)
354.335214 Prevention and control of pollution by local government (354.335 + 214)
354.3352140994 Prevention and control of pollution by local government in Australia (354.335 + 214 + 0994)

There is one major exception to the use of standard subdivisions, namely, to provide shorter numbers at 351.3–351.9 for public administration in specific places, thus saving two digits (e.g., 351.51 instead of 351.0951 for public administration in China).

560–590 LIFE SCIENCES

Why was a revision needed?

560–590 Life sciences was revised in DDC 21 because the old structure of the classification was fundamentally flawed. There are two different approaches to the study of biology:

- The study of internal processes in organisms in the laboratory: physiology, cytology, biochemistry, etc.; and

- The descriptive study of organisms in the field: ecology, taxonomy, etc.

The focus of study of internal processes is almost always the process before the taxonomic group. The biologist who studies the rat's brain in the laboratory is primarily interested in the brain; the species is incidental. However, the DDC used to scatter books on neurology (and other internal biological processes) by classing them with the taxonomic group first, and then adding a facet for the process. The revision in DDC Edition 21 reverses this, by putting the process first.

However, for the descriptive biological side—for what are called "external biological phenomena"—the primary focus remains with the taxonomic group. The revision here has concentrated on following more current taxonomic thinking, and on implementing the consequences of the switch in emphasis for internal processes.

Logical structure

In order to understand how the revision of 560–590 Life sciences works, you first need to understand the overall structure. In it you will see,

- Firstly, that the logical structure often works around the formal notation, in which every level is divided into ten at the next level; and

- Secondly, that to a large extent, within the new logical structure, many subjects keep the same notation. In particular, the taxonomic arrangement within 560 Paleontology, 580 Plants, and 590 Animals has not been revised as extensively as the topical arrangement within 570 Biology.

First level of classification

> 570 *Life sciences   Biology*
> > 560 *Paleontology   Paleozoology*
> > 571–575 *Internal biological processes*
> > 576–578 *General and external biological phenomena*
> > 579–590 *Natural history of specific kinds of organisms*

Second level of classification

> 570 *Life sciences   Biology*
> > 560 *Paleontology   Paleozoology*
> > > 561   *Paleobotany*
> > > 561.9 *Fossil microorganisms, fungi, algae*
> > > 562–569 *Specific taxonomic groups of animals*
> > 571–575 *Internal biological processes*
> > > 571   *Physiology and related subjects*
> > > 572   *Biochemistry*
> > > 573   *Specific physiological systems in animals*
> > > 575   *Specific parts of and physiological systems in plants*
> > 576–578 *General and external biological phenomena*
> > > 576   *Genetics and evolution*
> > > 577   *Ecology*
> > > 578   *Natural history of organisms*
> > 579–590 *Natural history of specific kinds of organisms*
> > > 579   *Microorganisms, fungi, algae*
> > > 580   *Plants*
> > > 590   *Animals*

Order of preference for complex topics

In 571–575: under last topic in schedule.

Between topic in 571–575 and topic in 579–590: choose 571–575.

Between topic in 576–578 and topic in 579–590: choose 579–590.

Faceting

Basically, there are four methods of faceted notation for complex subjects in 570–590 in Edition 21 of the DDC:

(i)   For genetics, evolution, ecology, and descriptive biology of specific taxonomic groups in 579–590.

(ii) For internal biology of specific taxonomic groups in 571–575.

(iii) For the combination of two aspects of internal biology in 571.5–571.9, 573, and 575.

(iv) For the combination of a general topic in biochemistry with a specific compound or group of compounds in 572.5–572.8.

An explanation of each method follows.

(i) GENETICS, EVOLUTION, ECOLOGY, AND DESCRIPTIVE BIOLOGY OF SPECIFIC TAXONOMIC GROUPS

The combination of topics in 576–578 with topics in 579–590 is carried out by using a faceted notation starting with "1" in 579–590. The instructions are at 579.2–579.8, 583–588, and 592–599 for specific taxonomic groups. The overall structure of the numbers added is:

—13 *Genetics and evolution (and young of animals in 592–599) [corresponding with 576 Genetics and evolution]*

—14 *Adaptation [corresponding with 578.4 Adaptation]*

—15 *Behavior (in 592–599) [corresponding with 591.5 Behavior]*

—16 *Miscellaneous nontaxonomic kinds [corresponding with 578.6 Miscellaneous nontaxonomic kinds of organisms]*

—17 *Plants/animals characteristic of specific environments, ecology [corresponding with 578.7 Organisms characteristic of specific kinds of environments and 577 Ecology]*

For example:

576.5 Genetics
579.135 Genetics of microorganisms
579.5135 Genetics of fungi
581.35 Genetics of plants
583.74135 Genetics of legumes
591.35 Genetics of animals
599.2135 Genetics of marsupials

This has meant that all numbers ending in "1" in 580 and 590 have had to be revised. For example, Monotremes has been moved from 599.1 in Edition 20 to 599.29 in Edition 21.

(ii) INTERNAL BIOLOGY OF SPECIFIC TAXONOMIC GROUPS

In 571–575, you find add instructions under:

> *571–572 Internal processes common to all organisms*
> *571.5–571.9 Tissue and cell biology, reproduction,*
> *   diseases, etc.*
> *572.5–572.8 Specific biochemicals and biochemical genetics*
> *573 Specific physiological systems in animals*
> *575 Specific parts of and physiological systems in plants*

In each of these cases (except 573, where notation 2 has a special meaning), you will find:

- notation "1" used for specific taxonomic groups of animals, divided like 590;

- notation "2" used for specific taxonomic groups of plants, divided like 580; and

- notation "29" used for specific taxonomic groups of micro-organisms, fungi and algae, divided like 579.

This is where Edition 21 implements a major change in the classification of the life sciences between Edition 20 and Edition 21 of the DDC. In Edition 20, internal processes in specific taxonomic groups were classed in 580–590, generally using standard subdivision —04 to add the facet for the internal process to the number for the taxonomic group. This meant that, for example, works on proteins were scattered through 574, 581–589, and 591–599. In Edition 21, they are brought together:

> *572.6 Proteins*
> *572.61 Proteins in animals*
> *572.6192 Proteins in marsupials*
> *572.62 Proteins in plants*
> *572.62374 Proteins in legumes*
> *572.629 Proteins in microorganisms*
> *572.6295 Proteins in fungi*

(iii) COMBINATION OF TWO ASPECTS OF INTERNAL BIOLOGY

Instructions on combining two aspects of internal biology are found at:

> *571.5–571.9 Tissue and cell biology, reproduction, diseases, etc.*
> *573 Specific physiological systems in animals*
> *575 Specific parts of and physiological systems in plants*
> *575.6–575.9 Reproductive organs and physiological systems in plants*

The instructions for these have some aspects in common, and some differences, which may be summarised in this way:

Meaning	Used in	Corresponds with
3 Anatomy and morphology application of one process to another	571.5–571.9, 573, 575	571.3–571.9
4 Biochemistry	573, 575.6–575.9	572

Note that the "Add to" instructions used for the faceting normally refer back to an earlier part of the schedule. This corresponds with the instruction at 571–575 to "class a subject with aspects in two or more subdivisions of 571–575 in the number coming last." This means that you can combine more than two aspects, for example:

> *571.3 Anatomy*
> *571.66 Nucleus*
> *571.6633 Anatomy of the nucleus [571.66 + 33]*
>
> *571.978 Tumors*
> *573.76 Bones*
> *573.763978 Bone tumors [573.76 + 3978]*
>
> *573.998 Appendages*
> *573.9983978 Tumors in appendages [573.998 + 3978]*

(iv) COMBINATION OF TWO TOPICS IN BIOCHEMISTRY

Instructions on combining two topics in biochemistry are found at:

572.5–572.8 Specific biochemicals and biochemical genetics

These instructions allow the combination of a topic in 572.3–572.4 with a topic in 572.5–572.8. They may be summarised in this way:

	Meaning	Used in	Corresponds with
3	General topics of biochemistry	572.5–572.8	572.3
4	Metabolism	572.5–572.8	572.4

Again, the "Add to" instructions used for the faceting normally refer back to an earlier part of the schedule, corresponding with the instruction at 571–575 to "class a subject with aspects in two or more subdivisions of 571–575 in the number coming last."

Reuse of numbers

When you have a major revision like 560–590 Life sciences, it is not always possible to avoid reusing numbers with a new meaning. For example, 578 means "Microscopy in biology" in Edition 20 and "Natural history of organisms" in Edition 21. However, the revision does avoid reusing numbers where large amounts of material have been classed in a typical library. The following numbers from Edition 20 are left vacant in Edition 21:

> 574 Biology
> 575.1 Genetics
> 575.2 Variation

In addition, 571, which will be heavily used in libraries using DDC 21, was unassigned in Edition 20, and was last used in Edition 16.

This will minimise the number of places where users will find material on different topics at the same number in those libraries that do not go back and reclassify older material.

Summary of the relocations in 570

For libraries planning to reclassify material, this is a summary of where material in 570 moves between Edition 20 and Edition 21:

Edition 20	*Edition 21*
570 Life sciences	570 Life sciences Biology
572 Human races	599.97–599.98 Human races
573 Physical anthropology	599.9 Hominidae Homo sapiens
574 Biology	570 Life sciences Biology
574.1 Physiology	571 Physiology
574.192 Biochemistry	572 Biochemistry
574.2 Pathology	571.9 Diseases Pathology
574.3 Development and maturation	571.8 Reproduction, development, growth
574.4 Anatomy and morphology	571.3 Anatomy and morphology
574.5 Ecology	577 Ecology
574.6 Economic biology	578.6 Miscellaneous nontaxonomic kinds of organisms
574.8 Tissue, cellular, molecular biology	571.5 Tissue biology and regional physiology
	571.6 Cell biology
	572.8 Biochemical genetics
574.9 Geographical treatment	578.09 Historical, geographic, persons treatment
	578.7 Organisms characteristic of specific kinds of environments
575 Evolution and genetics	576 Genetics and evolution
576 Microbiology	579 Microorganisms, fungi, algae
577 General nature of life	570.1 Philosophy and theory
578 Microscopy in biology	570.282 Microscopy
579 Collection and preservation of biological specimens	570.75 Museum activities and services Collecting

Relocations in 560, 580, and 590

The revision of 560 Paleontology, 580 Plants, and 590 Animals is much less extensive than that of 570 Life sciences. The schedules follow the same general classification by taxonomic groups, and still use 581 and 591 for general topics in plants and animals respectively. The main changes are:

- 581 and 591 have been extensively revised, with material relating to internal processes being relocated to 571–575.

- In 582–589 and 592–599, standard subdivision —04 is no longer used. Material that would be classed using —04 is relocated to 571–575 if it relates to internal processes. Otherwise, the new facet 1 is used.

- In 583–588 and 592–599, groups that were classed at numbers ending in 1 have been relocated to make room for the new facet.

- The parts of the schedule that have been most significantly revised are:

  583 Magnoliopsida (Dicotyledons)
  597.4–597.8 Actinopterygii (Ray-finned fishes); Amphibia
  599.3–599.9 Eutheria (Placental mammals)

These are groups with high literary warrant, but the revisions give a more logical arrangement and (in many cases) shorter numbers.

Dewey for Windows
Julianne Beall

INTRODUCTION

Dewey for Windows (DFW)[1] provides a Windows interface for the Dewey Decimal Classification (DDC). The DFW interface is different from the DOS version of Electronic Dewey, but the search engine (database access program) is similar.[2] This paper does not attempt to survey all the features of DFW; it focuses on those features that seem most important to the working classifier. It describes the hierarchies and the extra terminology for searching added to the DDC 21 database, search strategies, the limited number of built numbers in the database, and the need for number building. This paper also includes detailed descriptions of sample searches that illustrate how the system works.[3]

The Dewey for Windows database began as a database in the Editorial Support System (ESS) at the Library of Congress. The ESS format was developed before the MARC Format for Classification Data, but there are many similarities. For example, with both formats, a record contains a classification number, its caption, notes, and index entries. During development of the DDC 21 database, fields have been modified and information added to move the ESS format closer to the MARC format, so that eventually it will be easy to do machine conversion from ESS to MARC format.[4] Tapes written from the ESS database are used to produce both the print and the CD-ROM DDC. The CD-ROM version is produced by the OCLC Office of Research. A new CD-ROM is distributed every year at the same time that a new issue of *Dewey Decimal Classification, Additions, Notes and Decisions (DC&)* is published.

ADDITIONS TO THE DATABASE: HIERARCHIES AND EXTRA TERMINOLOGY

To each schedule and table record has been added the upward and downward hierarchy. For example, here is the hierarchy display for 796.5 Outdoor life:

```
   700   The arts    Fine and decorative arts
   790      Recreational and performing arts
   796         Athletic and outdoor sports and games
 > 796.5        Outdoor life
   796.51          Walking
   796.52          Walking and exploring by kind of terrain
   796.53          Beach activities
   796.54          Camping
   796.56          Dude ranching and farming
   796.58          Orienteering [formerly 796.51]
```

The hierarchy display makes it easy to ascertain the disciplinary context of a number and to see what its major subdivisions are. It is easy to move quickly up and down the hierarchy by highlighting and clicking.

Library of Congress subject headings have been added to the database by statistical matching. A set of bibliographic records with DDC 20 numbers from the Library of Congress was analyzed by computer, and the subject headings appearing most frequently in a record with a particular DDC number were added to the record for that Dewey number, up to five subject headings per record. These headings provide additional terms for searching. For example, the subject heading "Stage flying" was added by statistical matching to the record for 792.024, the number for special effects in the theater. The subject heading "Thermopylae, Battle of, 480 B.C." was added to the record for 938.03 Persian Wars, 500–479 B.C. Classifiers in libraries that use *Library of Congress Subject Headings (LCSH)* or one of the international translations/adaptations of *LCSH* will no doubt find these additions more helpful than classifiers in libraries that do not, but all Dewey users will find the extra terms useful for searching.

Because these statistically mapped subject headings were not post-edited, there are some bad matches; classifiers must always use these subject headings with caution, checking carefully to be sure there is not a better number for the topic. In particular, since there is at present no database of bibliographic records with DDC 21 numbers, when a new number has been provided in DDC 21, the subject heading will still be attached to the old number. Thus the subject heading "Computer viruses" is attached to 005.8 Data security, the number used for computer viruses in DDC 20; but DDC 21 has a new, more specific number for the topic: 005.84 Computer viruses. The user who finds 005.8 by means of the subject heading must look further to find the best number, e.g., by clicking on the Hierarchy button to check the downward hierarchy for 005.8. The statistical matchings will be done annually, and as a database of bibliographic records with DDC 21 numbers is developed, the matches will improve. Meanwhile, because the subject headings can be misleading, they have not been included in the default basic index; they must be searched explicitly, either in separate searches or with Boolean combinations, e.g., *internet or su:internet.* The "su:" is an index label specifying the LCSH (Words) index.

Intellectual mapping of Library of Congress subject headings to DDC numbers, as distinct from statistical mapping, is very time consuming; doing it for the whole database has not been possible. Intellectual mapping has been done as far as feasible for the following areas with major changes: 351–354 Public administration, 370 Education, and 560–590 Life sciences. Intellectually mapped subject headings are marked with an asterisk. For example, in the public administration schedule, the LCSH "*Municipal government" was added to 352.16 Urban administration. In the elementary education schedule, the headings "*Environmental education," "*Environmental sciences—Study and teaching (Elementary)," and "*Natural history—Study and teaching (Elementary)" were added to 372.357 Nature study. The following headings were added to 577 Ecology: "*Animal-plant relationships," "*Ecological heterogeneity," and "*Species diversity."

Nonprint DDC Relative Index entries are another source of additional terms for searching. There is abundant room on the CD-ROM for additional index entries, while the size of the Relative Index in volume 4 of the print DDC must be severely restricted; only index entries considered essential can be included in the print version. Of the two DDC Index Terms in the record for 658.4052 Negotiation, only the first appears in the print DDC 21:

Negotiation—executive management
Negotiation in business—executive management

The nonprint index entry was inspired by the frequently used LCSH "Negotiation in business"; it helps the classifier who has that subject heading in mind to find the record more quickly. For example, a keyword search on *negotiation w2 business* (where "w2" is a proximity operator) gets one hit, while a keyword search on *negotiation* gets thirteen hits. Some nonprint index entries are simply alternate spellings of print index entries, e.g., "Breastfeeding" when the print entry has two words, "Breast feeding"; such alternatives are more important for keyword searching than for browsing in the print index. Some nonprint index entries are for topics with marginal literary warrant, e.g., the following language names attached to T6—9433 Northern Turkic languages: Khakass language, Shor language, Tofa language.

BUILT NUMBERS AND NUMBER BUILDING

There are some built numbers in the print Dewey, especially in the Relative Index, and those are present in DFW. For example, the built number 005.7136 appears in the Relative Index with the following index entries:

Microcomputers—communications—programs
Microcomputers—interfacing—programs

Similarly, the built number 946.08148 appears in the Relative Index with one entry:

Air warfare—Civil War (Spain)

Keyword access is helpful for finding these built numbers, since classifiers do not always know what the lead term will be in an alphabetical listing. A classifier with a book on air operations during the Spanish Civil War can use a keyword search for *civil war and spain* to retrieve the built number listed in print only under Air warfare.

The current Dewey for Windows has no built numbers, and no LCSH that match built numbers, except for the built numbers in the print DDC 21. In the future, we plan to add many more built numbers with high postings to Dewey for Windows, plus the matching LCSH. Meanwhile, searching in DFW is not like searching in a database full of bibliographic records with built Dewey numbers. Searches for complex topics that would find hits in a bibliographic database will often yield no hits in Dewey for Windows. The pieces needed to build the number to express the concept may be present in the DFW database, as well as the instructions for constructing the appropriate Dewey number; but they are probably not all in the same record. For example, a keyword search for *opera? libretto?* (where the question mark [?] is a truncation symbol for zero or one character) will yield no hits, because there is no record in the database for that concept; however, there is a number for operas at 782.1, a number for librettos at 780.268, and instructions for combining them at 782.1–782.4, to form the built number 782.10268. A keyword search for *opera?* or *libretto?* yields the numbers 780.268 and 782.1, and a look at the full record for 782.1 reveals the note: "Add as instructed under 782.1–782.4." In the future, DFW will provide special number-building help to the classifier, but for now number building with DFW is much like number building with the print Dewey.

BASIC DEWEY PRINCIPLES AND RULES

It is important for classifiers using DFW to remember the basic Dewey principles and rules presented in the Introduction to the Dewey Decimal Classification and the DDC Glossary. The introduction and glossary are found online as part of the DFW Help system. The rule of zero, for example, is relevant to the opera librettos example:

Rule of zero (DDC Glossary)
The rule instructing that subdivisions beginning with zero should be avoided if there is a choice between 0 and subdivisions beginning with 1–9 in the same position in the notation. Similarly, subdivisions beginning with 00 should be avoided when there is a choice between 00 and 0.

That rule leads a classifier to expect 782.1 to be preferred over 780.268; thus the classifier saves time by looking first for the add instruction in the 782.1 record rather than the 780.268 record.

DEWEY FOR WINDOWS INTERFACE

The Dewey for Windows interface uses single-function windows. If a number or term is dragged and dropped into a Search window, a search for that number or term will begin. If a Dewey number is dragged and dropped into a DDC Number (Display) window, the full record for that number will be displayed, including the caption, notes, Relative Index entries, and associated Library of Congress subject headings. If a schedule or table number is dragged and dropped into a DDC Pages window, a display will appear that shows the number in the context of neighboring numbers in a format much like that of the printed page. If a term is dragged and dropped into an Index window set for the Relative Index (Phrases) index, the appropriate portion of the Relative Index will be displayed in a format somewhat like that of the printed Relative Index.

The windows are arranged in tiled fashion to facilitate dragging and dropping from one window to the next. There are four standard views and four customizable views for the classifier to set. One of the standard views is the Search view, which features a half-screen Search window and a half-screen DDC Number (Display) window, tiled vertically (figure 1). Another standard view is the Browse view, which features a half-screen DDC Pages window (tiled vertically), plus a Search window and a DDC Number (Display) window (figure 2). A third standard view is the Scan view, which features a half-screen Index window (tiled vertically), plus a Search window and a DDC Number (Display) window (figure 3).

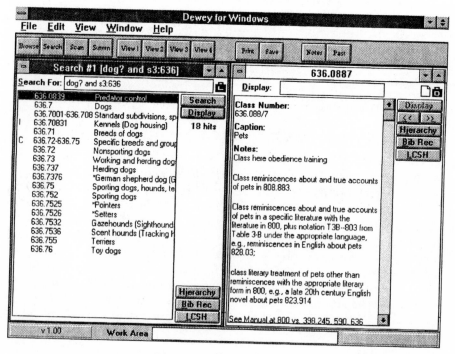

Figure 1: Search view

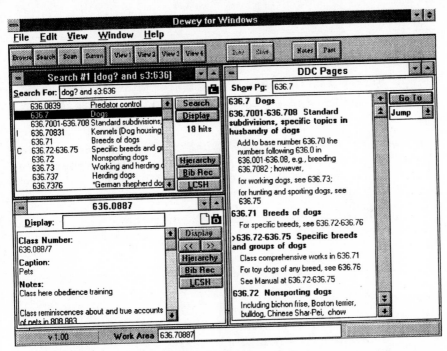

Figure 2: Browse view

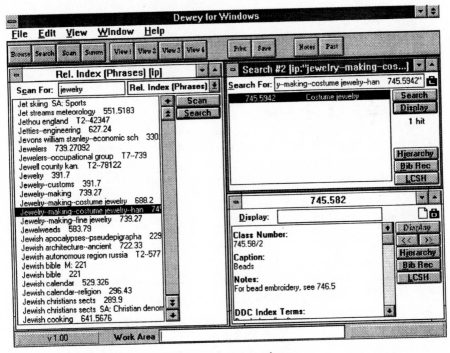

Figure 3: Scan view

Here are a few searches to show how the system works.

Sample Search #1: Obedience training for your pet dog

1. I begin with the Search view, which I activate by clicking on the Search button in the button bar at the top of the screen.

If I do a keyword search for *dog? and obedience training,* I get no hits; the built number for that concept is not in the database. The pieces and the instructions needed to build the number, however, are in the database.

I think that there may be many different numbers for dogs, but few if any for obedience training; hence I first try searching for obedience training.

2. In the input box of the Search window, I key: *obedience training*

Then I press the ENTER key.

3. With 636.0887 highlighted, I click on the Display button in the Search window to get a full record display.

Class Number:
636.088/7
Caption:
Pets
Notes:
Class here obedience training

. . . .

Now that I have found the number for obedience training of pets, I think that obedience training of pet dogs cannot be far away. Incidentally, for these sample searches I shall ignore all the segmentation marks (/) that indicate logical places to shorten numbers, because I plan to give unabridged numbers.

4. After double-clicking on "Search for:" to highlight for deletion the old text in the input box of the Search window, I key: *dog? and s3:636*

Then I press the ENTER key. The "s3:" is a restrictor specifying three significant digits; I am using it to limit my search results to DDC numbers beginning with the three digits 636.

5. I click on the Browse button in the button bar at the top of the screen to switch to the Browse view. The results of the previous searches are transferred from the Search window and DDC Number

(Display) window of the Search view to the corresponding windows of the Browse view. I want to use the half-screen DDC Pages window featured in the Browse view to help find any relevant add instructions, which may appear in subdivisions. The DDC Pages window has a compact display and facilitates browsing to nearby records. Remembering the rule of zero, I expect to find the add instruction associated with the main number for dogs (636.7) rather than with the number for obedience training of pets (636.0887).

6. In the Search window, I click on the line 636.7, drag it to the results area of the DDC Pages window and drop it. I find the add note I have been seeking in the record following 636.7.

636.7 Dogs
636.7001–636.708 Standard subdivisions, specific topics in husbandry of dogs
    Add to base number 636.70 the numbers following 636.0 in 636.001–636.08, e.g., breeding 636.7082

7. I highlight 636.70 in the add note, then drag the T suitcase containing the highlighted number from the top center of the screen to the Work Area at the bottom of the screen and drop it.

8. Following the add instruction, I add 887 from 636.0887 to the number in the Work Area to form the built number 636.70887. I can copy this built number to the Windows Notepad or elsewhere; I need not re-key it and risk introducing errors.

9. To avoid having to build this number over and over, I create a local note for it so that next time I can simply search my note file for *dogs—obedience training* or *636.70887*. In the notes field I can put any information that I might find helpful. Local notes are retained when a new CD-ROM is issued.

Sample Search #2: Ecology of a kelp bed

1. I click on the Search button in the button bar at the top of the screen to activate the Search view.

2. After highlighting for deletion the old text in the input box of the Search window, I key: *kelp?*

3. Two records match this query. With the first (333.9538 *Seaweeds) highlighted, I click on the Hierarchy button in the Search window.

```
300  Social sciences
330     Economics
333        Economics of land and energy
333.9        Other natural resources
333.95          *Biological resources
333.953            *Plants
> 333.9538             *Seaweeds
```

Economics is not the right discipline for the work. I press F2 to return to the standard Search view.

4. With "579.887 *Laminariales" highlighted, I click on the Hierarchy button in the Search window.

```
500  Natural sciences and mathematics
570     Life sciences    Biology
579        Microorganisms, fungi, algae
579.8        *Algae
579.88          *Phaeophyta (Brown algae)
> 579.887            *Laminariales
```

Biology is the right discipline, but still no sign of the correct subdiscipline: ecology. This book covers much more than just kelp; it treats all the creatures that live in and around kelp beds, from plankton to fishes to otters. I press F2.

5. In the input box of the Search window I key *su:* in front of my previous query and press ENTER to search for: *su:kelp?* The "su:" is an index label that specifies the LCSH (Word) index.

6. With " 577.78 %Nearshore ecology" highlighted, I drag the line to the results area of the DDC Number (Display) window and drop it to see the full record.

Class Number:
577.7/8
Caption:
%Nearshore ecology
Notes:
Class here sublittoral ecology
For saltwater wetland and seashore ecology, see 577.69
%Add as instructed under 577.76–577.79

DDC Index Terms:
Nearshore ecology
Sublittoral ecology
LC Subject Terms:
*Kelp bed ecology

I see that I have retrieved the record because of the LC Subject Term "*Kelp bed ecology." Because the heading has an asterisk (*), I know that it has been intellectually mapped to this number; hence, even though kelp bed ecology is a narrower topic than nearshore ecology or sublittoral ecology, I do not feel the need to check for a more specific subdivision. I assign 577.78 to the book.

Sample Search #3: How to make beaded bracelets

1. I begin by clicking on the Scan button in the button bar at the top of the screen to activate the Scan view, which features a half-screen Index window. I use the Index Selection box in the upper right corner of the Index window to select the Relative Index (Phrases).

2. In the input box of the Index window I key: *beads*
I press the ENTER key. The relevant and nearby entries are the following:

Bead embroidery   746.5
Beadle county s.d.   T2—783274
Beads   391.7
Beads—customs   391.7
Beads—handicrafts   745.582
Beads—home sewing   646.19
Beagle   636.7537

3. I highlight: Beads—handicrafts 745.582
Here I am using the Relative Index to help select the correct discipline: handicrafts.

4. I drag the highlighted line to the results area of the DDC Number (Display) window and drop it to see the full record.

Class Number:
745.58/2
Caption:
Beads
Notes:
For bead embroidery, see 746.5
DDC Index Terms:
Beads—handicrafts
LC Subject Terms:
Beadwork

5. After double-clicking on "Scan for:" in the Index window to highlight the old text for deletion, in the input box I key: *bracelets*

I click on the Scan button in the Index window (an alternative to pressing the ENTER key.) The relevant and nearby entries are the following:

Brabant belgium   T2—4933
Bracelets   391.7
Bracelets SA: Jewelry
Bracelets—customs   391.7
Bracelets—making   739.278
Brachiones   599.3583

I do not see a handicrafts number listed under Bracelets. I decide to follow the see-also reference to Jewelry.

6. I highlight the see-also reference: Bracelets SA: Jewelry

7. I drag that line to the Scan button in the Index window and drop it.

The relevant and nearby entries are the following:
Jewell county kan.   T2—78122
Jewelry   391.7
Jewelry—customs   391.7
Jewelry—making   739.27
Jewelry—making—costume jewelry   688.2
Jewelry—making—costume jewelry—han   745.5942
Jewelry—making—fine jewelry   739.27
Jewelweeds   583.79

8. I highlight: Jewelry—making—costume jewelry—han 745.5942

9. I drag the line to the Search window and drop it.

10. I click on the Browse button in the button bar at the top of the screen to activate the Browse view. I need to find out whether 745.582 or 745.5942 has preference. I will use the Browse view with its half-screen DDC Pages window to browse for preference information. When I change from the Scan view to the Browse view, the information in the Search and DDC Number (Display) windows transfers automatically to the corresponding windows in the Browse view.

11. I click on Hierarchy, highlight 745.5 Handicrafts, drag that line to the results area of the DDC Pages window and drop it. I use the Hierarchy display to get a sense of the context of the numbers and to move quickly to the number represented by the digits that the two possible choices have in common. That number is a good first place to look for preference information.

12. In the DDC Pages window I browse down to 745.51–745.58 Specific materials and read the first note: "Class specific objects made from specific materials in 745.59."

13. In the Search window I click on the Display button to see the full record for 745.5942. I need to check to be sure there is no problem with classing the book there.

Class Number:
745.594/2
Caption:
Costume jewelry
Notes:
Class interdisciplinary works on costume jewelry in 391.7;
class interdisciplinary works on making costume jewelry in 688.2; class interdisciplinary works on making jewelry in 739.27
DDC Index Terms:
Costume jewelry—handicrafts
Jewelry—making—costume jewelry—handicrafts
LC Subject Terms:
Jewelry making
Jewelry making—Juvenile literature
Beadwork
Polymer clay craft

14. I click on the Hierarchy button to make sure there is not a more specific subdivision for the book on bracelets.

700   The arts   Fine and decorative arts
740   Drawing and decorative arts
745   Decorative arts
745.5   Handicrafts
745.59   Making specific objects
745.594   Decorative objects
> 745.5942   Costume jewelry

There are no subdivisions. I assign 745.5942 to the book.

CONCLUSION

Keyword access to the entire DDC 21 corpus, additional terminology for searching, readily available hierarchy displays are all important advantages that Dewey for Windows offers to the classifier that are not available in the print Dewey. Another advantage is that the CD-ROM is always up-to-date without classifiers having to post changes from *DC&*. The need to understand basic Dewey principles and rules, however, remains the same as with the print DDC.

NOTES

1. Dewey for Windows, Version 1.00, OCLC Forest Press, Dublin, Ohio.

2. For descriptions of the DOS version, see Michael Carpenter, "Electronic Dewey, version 1.00 [review]," *Cataloging & Classification Quarterly* 19, no. 1 (1995): 134–37. See also Ross Trotter, "Electronic Dewey: The CD-ROM Version of the Dewey Decimal Classification," *Cataloging & Classification Quarterly* 19, no. 3/4 (1995): 213–34.

3. For additional information about Dewey for Windows, see Diane Vizine-Goetz and Mark Bendig, "Dewey for Windows: Accessing the Dewey Decimal Classification from the Technical Services Workstation," in *Planning and Implementing Technical Service Workstations*, ed. Michael Kaplan (Chicago: American Library Association, 1996). See also Julianne Beall, "Dewey for Windows," in *Knowledge Organization and Change: Proceedings of the 4th International ISKO Conference, 15–18 July 1996, Washington, D.C.*, ed. Rebecca Green (Frankfurt/Main: INDEKS Verlag, 1996), 396–405.

4. For more information about the Editorial Support System and its format, see John J. Finni and Peter J. Paulson, "The Dewey Decimal Classification Enters the Computer Age: Developing the DDC Database and Editorial Support System, *International Cataloguing* 16, no. 4 (Oct./Dec. 1987): 46–48. See also Julianne Beall, "Editing the Dewey Decimal Classification Online: The Evolution of the DDC Database," in *Classification Research for Knowledge Representation and Organization: Proceedings of the 5th International Study Conference on Classification Research, Toronto, Canada, June 24–28, 1991*, ed. Nancy J. Williamson and Michèle Hudon (Amsterdam and New York: Elsevier, 1992), 29–37.

The Dewey Decimal Classification System in National Bibliographies

Barbara L. Bell

INTRODUCTION

I am pleased to be included as part of this workshop. My contribution comes from my research and working with national bibliographies around the world, not from my expertise with the Dewey Decimal Classification system. With that disclaimer, I am ready to share my observations and experience in how national bibliographies and national bibliographic services use the DDC in national bibliographies, including a case study of the making of the *Namibia National Bibliography.*

WHAT IS A NATIONAL BIBLIOGRAPHY AND HOW IS IT USED?

So that we all begin at the same place, let me briefly define what it is that I mean when I use the words "national bibliography."

Recommendations from the International Congress on National Bibliographies, Paris 1977 (ICNB), state that countries around the world should establish a national agency responsible for collecting, under legal deposit legislation, the publishing output of that country, producing authoritative and comprehensive records of these publications, and publishing a bibliography of national imprints in a timely fashion. Recommendations from this conference have become guidelines for nations who are responsible for national bibliographies.[1] More recently, in the more technologically advanced countries of the world, national bibliographies have expanded beyond the printed bibliography to other formats and services.

A current national bibliography reflects the character and culture of a nation as well as the history of the nation as it records its publishing output. Events which have an impact on a nation should find their way into the national imprint; in this way, history is recorded, recalled, and remembered.

I will address why a national bibliography is arranged in a classified order; what classification systems are used; which countries use the DDC; how the DDC is used, including policies, problems, benefits of selected countries which use the DDC; and how classification number access can vary according to the format of the national bibliography. I will conclude with a case study of the *Namibia National Bibliography*, which highlights both the benefits and problems in using the DDC and provides insight into specific applications of the DDC.

WHY IS A NATIONAL BIBLIOGRAPHY ARRANGED IN A CLASSIFIED ORDER?

Most users of national bibliographies come seeking information for a specific reason, and most are best served by an organized subject approach.

The ICNB Recommendation number 11 states:

The current issues of the printed national bibliography should be arranged in a classified order in accordance with a stated internationally-used classification scheme and the arrangement of cumulations should be decided at the discretion of the national bibliographic agency . . .

ICNB Recommendation number 10 suggests that an outline of the classified arrangement (if used) should be given in the introduction.

The recommendations do not prescribe which classification to use; that decision is left to each country. However, it is important to arrange the publications of a country during a particular time period in some logical, internationally recognized manner so that the information is accessible to those who use national bibliographies, and so that this system can be explained to the user.

WHAT CLASSIFICATION SYSTEMS OR ORGANIZATIONAL SCHEMES ARE USED MOST OFTEN?

National bibliographies are organized by systems that fall into four broad categories. The largest number of countries use the Dewey Decimal Classification system. The second most often used classification system is the Universal Decimal Classification. The third category includes those countries that use their own national system, have modified another internationally recognized system, such as the DDC or the Library of Congress Classification system, or use broad subject categories in their national bibliography. Finally, the fourth category I refer to as "Other." These countries may have no classification number given in the entry information but are alphabetically arranged by main entry, or organized first chronologically by imprint date, and then alphabetically.

Parenthetically I will mention that there are a few countries that include two classification numbers for each entry in the information that is given. Canada, India, and the Philippines are three examples.

For a list of national bibliographies and the organizing scheme that each uses, see table 1.

WHICH COUNTRIES USE THE DDC?

In my ongoing research to locate, describe, and analyze national bibliographies, first for my 1986 *An Annotated Guide to Current National Bibliographies*, and most recently for the upcoming second edition planned for 1997, part of the information examined is the classification system used in various national bibliographies. Of the 108 national bibliographies or suitable substitutes found and described in the 1986 edition, 55 countries (or over half) use the Dewey Decimal Classification system. Three additional countries arrange the entries using DDC headings although they list no classification number in their national bibliography. I am updating information for my revised editon and have included changes in table 1 as I have discovered them. Broken into broad geographic categories, 17 are from African countries, 13 are from the Americas/Caribbean, 9 are from Asian countries, the Middle East has 7, and Pacific/Oceania and Europe have 6 each. Please refer to table 2 for this geographic breakdown.

Another group of countries use their own decimal classification system: Danish Decimal Classification, Nippon Decimal Classification, Liechtenstein Decimal Classification, Taiwan Central Library Classification—a few of which are closely related to the DDC system.

As I continue to update information, these numbers will change and there are likely to be additional national bibliographies that will have organized or enhanced their product with the DDC. One example is the *Ghana National Bibliography*. In the 1980s, it was organized by broad subject headings; now it uses the DDC. Another is Namibia. The suitable substitute for its national bibliography in 1986 used subject headings but had no classification numbers. Now Namibia's first national bibliography, published in 1996, uses the DDC. The Philippines have added the DDC number to their national bibliography. If any of you are aware of countries I have not included in table 1, please let me know. With the translation of the DDC into several languages, there may be some other countries that decide to use this system in their national bibliographies. There also will be national bibliographies in a suspended state because of political or economic reasons. Guyana is one example. These changes will be recorded as I complete my research.

HOW IS THE DDC USED IN NATIONAL BIBLIOGRAPHIES?

One of the strengths of the DDC is the versatility in how it can be used to organize information. A country is free to choose what works best for its libraries—close or broad classification. This depends on the size of the collection, the need for specificity and detail, and the DDC needs of the libraries that depend upon the national bibliographic agency or national library.

In national bibliographies, the DDC is used to organize the entries in the main body, and many times DDC numbers appear in a subject index. The DDC number may be the link from the index to the main body of information.

Countries may choose to use suitable designations or codes in combination with the DDC to classify for local use literature and languages that are important to that country. If this is done, these designations will be explained in the introductory remarks.

In preparation for this presentation, I wrote to several editors of national bibliographies that use the DDC asking them to share: 1) policies they have with regard to the DDC; 2) problems they have encountered with the DDC; 3) ways in which the DDC has been beneficial to their national bibliography; and 4) how technology has affected their use of the DDC.[2] I will share a number of responses to these areas under the headings of policies, problems, and benefits:

Policies

The *British National Bibliography* (*BNB*) has used the DDC since the *BNB* was first published in 1950. According to Mr. Ross Trotter of the British Library it was never questioned that this be so. The DDC is used in almost all of the public libraries and educational institutions in the United Kingdom. The use of the DDC in the *BNB* has ensured continued use of the DDC in the United Kingdom.

South Africa has restricted the classification number length to nineteen digits, excluding the decimal. This policy affects in particular class numbers 496 and 896 when the Fivaz and Scott tables are used.[3]

Both the British Library and the State Library (South Africa) stated that it is the policy of their library to adopt the most current edition of the DDC. The British Library looks forward to a trial period with Dewey for Windows; the State Library (South Africa) is looking forward to acquiring DDC 21 in electronic format.

The State Library (South Africa) does not do retrospective reclassification when new DDC editions are published. Its library collection is not shelved according to subject; therefore, it doesn't require rearrangement on the shelf.

The *New Zealand National Bibliography* and its predecessors have used the current editions of the DDC since 1960. The DDC was first applied to monographs, and as of 1983, it has been applied to serials. For geographical designations, the DDC has been adapted using O'Reilly numbers. The DDC 21 changes in Tables 2, 5, and 6 will allow for the new geographic designations in New Zealand.

Problems

While the State Library (South Africa) does not reclassify, Mr. Trotter of the British Library states that extensively revised schedules cause tension when customers are unwilling to accept the need for reclassification. When a collection is organized by subject, then a library has to decide how it is that they will reflect that change. Most often, there is a need for reclassification.

The tension between local need and international standardization was illustrated well by Mr. Trotter. He cites the example of the 340 Law schedule. In 1981 the British Library chose Option B, which arranges law by jurisdiction. The Library of Congress regularly supplied Option B numbers—that is, until DDC 21. It is likely that the British Library now will revert to the preferred order rather than continue with their choice of Option B.

Several African countries mentioned the need to use amended DDC numbers, particularly for languages in 496 and literatures in 896. African countries need to bring more specificity to African languages and literatures. One number each in the 400s and in the

800s is provided for all of Africa, and there may be over twenty different languages and dialects within one particular country. In South Africa, the Fivaz and Scott tables are used to provide distinctive identification to the literature and language sections specific to South Africa. Namibia explored the use of these tables but found that several dialects were not included in these tables. Namibia decided to use unique three-character language designations attached to the DDC number, which have the approval or are awaiting the approval of the Library of Congress. Ms. Mulindwa of the Botswana National Library Services (BNLS) states that in northern Botswana Ikalanga is a spoken and written language that is quite different from Setswana. It would be wrong to classify the two together under one number. In these categories, the DDC does not go far enough, and is not as specific as it needs to be for African countries (non-Western cultures).

Long numbers were mentioned as a problem by several countries, again predominately by African countries, and particularly by southern African countries that are an extension of the number for South Africa. Botswana and Namibia, both independent countries, require the addition of four numbers when country specificity is required, e.g., Namibia is 6881.

Ms. Mulindwa mentioned that at times the *National Bibliography of Botswana* will assign a primary DDC number and a second DDC classification number when number building does not seem adequate to bring out necessary subjects.

Mr. Trotter mentioned a lack of specificity in earlier editions of the DDC, which resulted in many titles under a single class number and made searching for particular titles difficult. To solve this problem, in the 1960s Britain created its own expansions using lower case letters added to class numbers (e.g., 656pmq for Airports). This created its own set of problems. Although this has now ceased in current practice and the *BNB* supplies the authoritative DDC number for the country, local libraries may choose to amend when necessary.

Ms. Kellerman of the State Library (South Africa) mentioned that this lack of specificity continues to be a problem for subjects either unique to South Africa or treated differently than suggested in the DDC. She gives several examples: minibus taxis; NGOs are neither charities nor international organizations in South Africa; the African concept of family is different from that suggested in the DDC; government structure is different; internal changes (political developments, new provinces) are not accommodated; and the term "minority" implies disadvantaged whereas in South Africa, the disadvantaged are the majority. Therefore, numbers such as 338.6422 (minority enterprises) cannot be used.

Ms. Rollitt, National Library of New Zealand, indicated their desire to separate literary works by a single author from history, criticism, and biographies of the author and his/her works. They have decided to add a "B" for biographies as LC does, but the history and criticism still remain with the literature.

New Zealand would like to see more LC subject headings included in the DDC index; since the DDC and Library of Congress subject headings are often used together, it would make life easier!

Benefits

Both Ms. Kellerman, State Library (South Africa) and Ms. Mulindwa, BNLS, mentioned the helpfulness of the Manual in decision making for creating DDC numbers. Its guidance helps provide consistency and clarity.

When a national bibliography uses the DDC, it influences the use of the DDC in libraries within the country, and provides a point of reference and guidance for both cataloging and classification. It helps provide a consistency within the country.

Each edition of the DDC improves on the coverage of subject areas from previous editions, states Ms. Mulindwa.

Several major national bibliographies use the DDC. When in doubt about a number, one can refer to these bibliographies to see how similar titles were treated.

When DDC headings for DDC numbers are added to library databases, they have proved to be useful to the staff of the State Library (South Africa) and to the National Library of Namibia.

CLASSIFICATION NUMBER ACCESS CAN VARY ACCORDING TO THE FORMAT OF THE NATIONAL BIBLIOGRAPHY

In printed bibliographies, the main body of information, with few exceptions, is always organized in some classification sequence, with additional access to information through various indexes that refer back to the main entry using either the national bibliography sequence number or the classification number.

Microfiche editions may not have this visible access via a classification system. The register or main body of information is recorded as the material is received, with additional access points to subject headings or titles or authors also provided. The classification number is given as part of the register information, but may not be accessible in any other way except as it parallels the categories one consults in a subject index.

National bibliographies on CD-ROM usually have a search capability that allows the user to generate a list by subjects, keywords, or classification numbers, as well as by other useful categories. If one is interested in finding all publications in the latest CD-ROM under the classification number 636, for example, then one asks for a search on the 636 number. If the CD-ROM is cumulative, the results will yield all of the publications under that number; it may be possible to limit the search to the latest year.

Computer-generated products such as magnetic tapes can be manipulated to produce reports for various categories, of which classification lists would be one option.

NAMIBIA NATIONAL BIBLIOGRAPHY (NNB): A CASE STUDY

In 1990, Namibia became an independent country, ending its era of administrative rule by South Africa. The National Library wanted to begin its own national bibliography starting from independence. In 1994, through the American Library Association Library Fellow program, I was asked to go to Namibia for nine months to help the library staff establish standards, guidelines, and procedures for their new national bibliography. I stayed for ten months as an ALA Library Fellow and then returned for six weeks under the USIA Academic Specialist program in the summer of 1995 to help with the bibliography. These visits turned out to be an opportunity of a lifetime for me. After analyzing and describing national bibliographies during the previous ten years, I was given the opportunity to help create an internationally acceptable national bibliography from its beginning.

As one would assume, a lot of preparatory work needed to be done before the project could get off the starting line. One important aspect was my receiving training in CDS/ISIS, the UNESCO system. A decision to use CDS/ISIS for the national bibliography was made at the Undersecretary level shortly after I arrived. This system was free to developing countries, a resident expert could train other librarians to use the system, and several libraries in Namibia were using this system already.

A decision as to the classification system to be used in organizing the bibliography was made in consultation with the director and librarians. The DDC is widely used in Namibian libraries and was the top choice for the *NNB*. That decision was the easy part!

The National Library's Namibiana collection, the group of material that was to make up the bulk of the national bibliography, is housed in a closed shelving area and is arranged by accession number. None of the titles in the Namibiana collection had been assigned a classification number to indicate subject. A database of the Namibiana material is maintained by Werner Hildebrecht, a former staff member at the National Archives, now at the National Library of Namibia. This database, NAMLIT, has a wider scope than that needed for the national bibliography; lists the serials housed in the National Archives rather than in the National Library; and operates on a system incompatible with CDS/ISIS. However, it was decided that the NAMLIT record was the place to begin creating a national bibliographic record for the *NNB* database. A project to convert NAMLIT records to UNIMARC records for use on CDS/ISIS was launched in March and ended in August, eight months into my ten-month stay.

Much could be done while waiting for the database conversion; the sad part is that whatever was done could not be entered into the database until the conversion was completed. Enhancement of the records for 1990–1992 monographs (the time period covered in the first issue) required the addition of Library of Congress subject headings, Dewey Decimal Classification numbers, and AACR2 descriptions. It was decided that this first issue would include all serials currently received by the National Library that were still in existence in 1992. An inventory was needed to determine title changes, and to note other changes. With the country name officially changed from South West Africa to Namibia, there were many serials that required new entries during this period. The National Library does not classify nor catalog their periodicals or newspapers. Therefore, a lot of preparatory work was required before an authoritative record could be included in the *NNB* database.

In using the DDC, Namibia decided to use close classification. Admittedly, this decision leads to some rather long numbers, but it was felt that libraries should have the option to be specific if needed. The National Library sets the standards for other libraries in the country, which have a variety of needs. We wanted to be as precise as possible. If individual Namibian libraries want to use broader classification numbers, that could be their choice. It is easier for libraries to go from a close number to a broad number rather than the other way around.

One of the problems we had was how to treat annual reports. Most places using the DDC with which I was familiar did not classify annual reports. However, we wanted to include them in the national bibliography and therefore these reports needed numbers. They needed to be treated consistently. It was unclear whether they should be treated as serials (—05) or as administrative reports from profit and nonprofit organizations and companies (—06). Fortunately, before going to Namibia, I made contact with Joan Mitchell, editor of the Dewey Decimal Classification and asked her for guidance. After discussing this point with the Decimal Classification Editorial Policy Committee, Ms. Mitchell recommended that —05 be used for classifying annual reports in all places except the 350s, and when Edition 21 was published, the 350s could be included.

For literature and for language publications, we found we needed greater specificity than what was available in the DDC. There are many indigenous languages and dialects in Namibia (see table 3). (It was interesting to me that at least two publishers were sponsoring contests for the best poetry or short story in a particular indigenous language. The publishers rotated the contests among major indigenous languages annually. The winner would have his/her work published. Such encouragement to write in indigenous languages has continued since independence.) After conferring with colleagues in several countries, we decided to adopt the three-letter designation used in the NAMLIT database. This list of designations had been approved by the Library of Congress a few years earlier. A second list is still pending approval. By using these designations, we were able to indicate the specific dialect of the language group, thus pulling together books on like languages and literatures. This enhancement is noted in the introduction to the *NNB*.

Examples of a 496 and an 896 entry using the three-letter codes are as follows:

496.39982ndo
Viljoen, Johannes Jurgens
Okwiilonga elaka : embo lyokwiilonga Oshindonga. 4 / J. Viljoen, P. Amakali. - Windhoek : Gamsberg Macmillan, 1991.
93 p. : ill. ; 21 cm.
Text in Ndonga
ISBN 0-86848-040-1 (pbk)
LCSH: Ndonga language—Grammar ; Ndonga language—Text-books.
AE: Amakali, Petrus, 1937–
F001 : 93/1014 A

896.399321oz
Muyunda, Charles Walubita, 1952–
Utwa muhaesu / Charles Walubita Muyunda. - Windhoek : Gamsberg Macmillan, 1992.
106 p. ; 21 cm.
Text in Lozi.
First published 1990 by Kenneth Kaunda Foundation, Lusaka.
ISBN 1-86848-773-3 (pbk)
LCSH: Lozi fiction
F001 : 92/1401 A

The irritation that newly independent Namibia is classified as an extension of the South Africa DDC number came up periodically. This feeling is not unique to Namibia. Many of the southern Africa countries feel that since they are independent countries now, they would prefer to have their own number rather than be classified as an extension of South Africa's number. If this is not addressed in Edition 21, it should be addressed in the next edition.

In pursuing a unique number for Namibia, I again wrote to Joan Mitchell. She listed four criteria that need to be met for a country to have its unique number (or further expansion): 1) a stable political situation; 2) cooperation of the national library and/or national library association; 3) availability of authoritative maps; and 4) literary warrant in the LC and OCLC online catalog databases. The first three criteria have been met. With the new national bibliography, it will be easier to determine the number of publications for Namibia in a year and also increase the chances of a title's availability to determine the fourth criterion. Many of these titles have small print runs and publications are not widely distributed outside of the country. The Library of Congress Field Office located in Kenya has helped LC get several of these publications and thus has given the publications wider exposure through the LC bibliographic information distributed through various databases such as OCLC. This exposure will also be aided by the publication of the national bibliography.

For Namibia's purposes, the DDC works well in organizing the *Namibia National Bibliography.* The National Library is establishing authority records for publications that have not previously been either cataloged or classified. As a result, more libraries internally will use the DDC to organize their collections. It is ironic that the National Library's Namibiana collection remains in accession order on the library shelves, not in DDC order, while the DDC is used in the national bibliography, is provided in the *NNB* database, and is accessible through the LAN for the reference librarian's use. Only through using the national bibliography or NAMLIT does one know how many books the library has on a certain subject or in a particular language.

The first edition of *NNB* includes 1028 titles published from 1990–1992 in Namibia or about Namibia, including all serials currently received by the library regardless of beginning date. In subsequent issues only new and ceased titles, or serials with title changes, will be listed. The next issue, to cover 1993–1995, is in process. It is planned that with the 1996 volume, the *NNB* will become an annual publication. By recording the legal deposit receipts of the National Library of Namibia, the *NNB* is sharing the publishing output of Namibia with scholars, bibliographers, government officials, and librarians around the world. Through its contribution to national bibliographic control, it will aid in international bibliographic control. And because of the DDC, users will be able to access subjects quickly.

CONCLUSION

The DDC is widely used in national bibliographies throughout the world and its use is increasing. It allows easy access by subject to users of national bibliographies. Benefits include international as well as local cooperation and consistency. Problems, particularly for non-Western countries, include a different definition of subjects, or a lack of specificity of subjects, literatures, and languages as expressed through Edition 20. Perhaps future editions will address some of these problems. Examples from the British Library, State Library (South Africa), National Library of Namibia, Botswana National Library Service, National Library of New Zealand, and National Library (Guyana) illustrate uses of the DDC in current national bibliographies. A case study of the *Namibia National Bibliography* discusses both the benefits and problems of using the DDC. Two accompanying tables show the extent to which the DDC is used worldwide in national bibliographies. A third table lists the numerous languages found in Namibia, thus illustrating difficulties in having one number available to classify African languages and literatures.

NOTES

1. See International Congress on National Bibliographies (Paris, 12–15 Sept. 1977). *Final Report.* (PGI/77/UBC/3). This information also appears in Barbara L. Bell, *An Annotated Guide to Current National Bibliographies* (Alexandria, Va. and Cambridge, Eng.: Chadwyck-Healey, 1986), 403–7.

2. Countries written to were Botswana, Canada, Great Britain, Guyana, Iceland, India, Kenya, Namibia, New Zealand, South Africa, Trinidad & Tobago, and Turkey. My thanks go to the detailed comments and responses of Barbara Kellerman, State Library (South Africa); Ross Trotter, British Library; Louise Hansmann, National Library of Namibia; G.K. Mulindwa, Botswana National Library Service; Karen Rollitt, National Library of New Zealand; and Gwyneth Browman, National Library (Guyana).

3. Since the 1970s, the State Library (South Africa) has used the Fivaz and Scott tables to distinguish between the various indigenous languages. The bibliographic citation is D. Fivaz and P.E. Scott, *African Languages: A Genetic and Decimalised Classification for Bibliographic and General Reference* (Boston: G.K. Hall, 1977).

Table 1

National Bibliographies/Suitable Substitutes That Use the DDC and Those That Use Other Organizing Schemes•

Dewey Decimal Class.	Dewey Decimal Class.	Universal Decimal Class.	Other Class./ Subject	No Class.; Arranged by Alphabet, Chronology, Language
Australia	Malaysia	Albania	Austria	Ethiopia
Bangladesh	Malta	Algeria	Belgium	Honduras
Barbados	Mexico	Benin	Canada +	Hong Kong
Bermuda	Namibia *	Bulgaria	China	Mauritius
Bolivia	Nepal	Czech Republic	Costa Rica	Netherlands
Botswana	New Zealand	Ecuador	Cuba	Puerto Rico
Brazil	Nigeria	Finland	Denmark	
Canada +	Norway	France	Dominican Republic	
Chile	Pakistan	Germany #	India +	
Colombia **	Palestine	Hungary	Israel	
Egypt	Papua New Guinea	Madagascar	Ivory Coast	
Fiji	Peru	Morocco	Japan	
The Gambia	Philippines +	Poland	Korea	
Ghana *	Qatar	Portugal	Liechtenstein	
Greece	Sierra Leone	Romania	Luxembourg	
Guyana	Singapore	Russia	Philippines +	
Iceland	South Africa	Senegal		
India +	Sri Lanka	Slovakia	Sudan	
Indonesia	Swaziland	Spain	Sweden	
Iran	Syria	Tunisia	Switzerland	
Iraq	Tanzania	Yugoslavia	Taiwan	
Ireland	Thailand		United States	
Italy	Trinidad & Tobago		Uruguay	
Jamaica	Turkey		Vietnam	
Jordan	United Kingdom			
Kenya	Venezuela			
Laos	Zaire			
Libya	Zambia			
	Zimbabwe			

•Based on 1986 research for *An Annotated Guide to Current National Bibliographies*. Revision is in progress for the second edition; new information known as of April 1996 is included. Notably missing is information from the Commonwealth of Independent States, and the Baltic countries.

+ One of two classifications provided.

* Changed to the DDC since 1986 research.

** Uses DDC headings but no classification numbers.

Before unification, the GDR used the Soviet BBK; since unification, the Federal Republic of Germany uses the 10 main headings of the UDC.

Table 2
Geographic Breakdown for National Bibliographies/ Suitable Substitutes That Use the DDC

Africa	Americas/ Caribbean	Asia/ South Asia	Europe	Middle East	Pacific/ Oceania
Botswana	Barbados	Bangladesh	Greece	Iran	Australia
Egypt	Bermuda	India	Iceland	Iraq	Fiji
Gambia	Bolivia	Laos	Ireland	Jordan	Indonesia
Ghana	Brazil	Malaysia	Italy	Palestine	New Zealand
Kenya	Canada	Nepal	Norway	Qatar	Papua New Guinea
Libya	Chile	Pakistan	United Kingdom	Syria	Philippines
Malawi	Colombia	Singapore		Turkey	
Malta	Guyana	Sri Lanka			
Namibia	Jamaica	Thailand			
Nigeria	Mexico				
Sierra Leone	Peru				
South Africa	Trinidad & Tobago				
Swaziland	Venezuela				
Tanzania					
Zaire					
Zambia					
Zimbabwe					

Table 3
NAMLIT Language Codes for Use in the *Namibia National Bibliography*

Language	3-Letter Code	Language Group	Additional Information	Defined by LC Code
Afrikaans	afr	European		yes
/=Akhoe	akh	Khoisan	San language	no
Dciriku (Gciriku, Rugciriku)	gci	Bantu	Kavango	no
Dhimba (Cimba)	dhi	Bantu	Herero dialect in Kunene	no
English	eng	European		yes
Fwe	fwe	Bantu	Caprivi	no
German	ger	European		yes
Hai//omn	*	Khoisan	Khoekhoe dialect	no
Herero	her	Bantu	Herero language	yes
Korana	kra	Khoisan	extinct	no
!Ko	*	Khoisan	San language from Nosob area	no
!Kung	kun	Khoisan	San language, including Ju/wa dialect	no
Kwambi	kwb	Bantu	Ovambo	no
Kwangali	kwa	Bantu	Kavango	no
Kwanyama	kua	Bantu	Ovambo dialect	yes
Kxoé	kxo	Khoisan	San language, in Kavango	no
Lozi	loz	Bantu	Caprivi/Zambia/Zimbabwe	yes
Mbanderu	*	Bantu	Herero dialect in Omaheke	no
Mbukushu	mbk	Bantu	Kavango	no
Mbunza	*	Bantu	Kavango	no
Khoekhoe Gowab**	nam	Khoisan	Southern/Central Namibia	yes
Ndonga	ndo	Bantu	Ovambo dialect	yes
Nharo	nha	Khoisan	San language	no
Ovambo(unspecified)	ova	Bantu	With expert input, most entries could be allocated to Ndonga or Kwanyama	no
Sambiu	*	Bantu	Kavango	no
Subia	sub	Bantu	Caprivi	no
Totela	tot	Bantu	Caprivi	no
Tswana	tsw	Bantu	Omaheke region	yes

* No published material to date that warrants a code.
** Formerly Nama/Damara.

The DDC in the Asia-Pacific Region
Giles S. Martin

INTRODUCTION

To describe how the Dewey Decimal Classification is used in the Asia-Pacific region is an enormous task. In my paper I will be able to do little more than summarise the situation, perhaps providing a few highlights that may illuminate general trends.

The Asia-Pacific region, if it is defined as including East Asia, South Asia, Southeast Asia, and the Pacific region, is an area which includes more than half the population of the world—more than three billion people.

There are wide differences in the region:

- In economic development, with the region including advanced industrial economies like Australia, Japan, and Singapore, and less developed economies, that have been held back by colonialism and war;

- In cultures, with the region including countries with ancient civilisations such as those of China, India, and Japan, and countries strongly influenced by Western European and North American civilisation;

- In general levels of education, particularly literacy rates, which vary from country to country in the region from 20 percent to nearly 100 percent; and

- In languages: Across the region, a large variety of languages are used, and even within some countries (such as India and Papua New Guinea) there may be dozens or even hundreds of different languages.

Not only do these factors make it difficult to generalise about the region, but these factors all affect the development of libraries in general, and the library classification schemes used in particular.

CULTURAL IMPERIALISM OR TECHNOLOGY TRANSFER?

Some of the earliest libraries in the world started in this region—particularly in China, where the earliest libraries existed long before the library at Alexandria. However, during the last hundred years or so, most innovations in library practice have originated in North America or in Western Europe. This reflects the economic predominance of those regions—an economic predominance that is, of course, now being challenged by the Asia-Pacific Region.

In particular, there has been a strong influence from the United States, Britain, and Australia on library practice in the Asia-Pacific region. This has involved librarians from the region going to library schools overseas, and librarians from other countries carrying out training and consultancies in the region. Of course, this imported practice is then modified by local needs and local traditions.

As part of this general trend, the Dewey Decimal Classification has been adopted widely in the region, following practice in the United States, Britain, and Australia, where libraries adopted the DDC early and extensively. Ironically, in areas where United States influence has been strongest in library practice, the Library of Congress Classification (LCC) has been adopted widely since the 1960s, particularly in academic libraries, following the move towards LCC in the United States.

Another influence on classification practice has been the wide availability of DDC numbers from centralised sources—including LC printed cards, LC MARC records, and national bibliographies (which are often modelled on the *British National Bibliography*). These sources may include other classification schemes as well, such as the LC Classification on LC cards and in LC MARC records.

NATIONAL BIBLIOGRAPHIES

Because national bibliographies provide an easily usable source of cataloguing data, they have a strong influence on cataloguing and classification practice. Thus, a summary of classification practice in national bibliographies in the region will help explain classification practice in the various countries in the region.

Many national bibliographies are modelled, either directly or indirectly, on the *British National Bibliography*, which is arranged in DDC order. Thus, most have a classified arrangement, and in most of these, the classification used is the DDC:

Bangladesh	Modified DDC
China	Classification scheme for Chinese libraries
Fiji	DDC
India	DDC; also uses Colon Classification
Indonesia	Expanded DDC
Malaysia	DDC
Nepal	DDC
New Zealand	DDC
Pakistan	DDC
Papua New Guinea	Expanded DDC
Philippines	DDC
Singapore	DDC
South Korea	Korean Decimal Classification
Sri Lanka	DDC
Thailand	DDC

This gives a picture of the DDC being used in national bibliographies wherever they exist in the Asia-Pacific region, with the exception of East Asia—China, Japan, and Korea—where other classification schemes predominate. This is a pattern that is repeated in library practice, as we will see later.

AUSTRALIA

I will start by discussing the use of the DDC in Australia, for at least three reasons:

- I know more about Australia than about any other country, since I come from there.

- Australia was the first country in the region to use the Dewey Decimal Classification.

- Australia has been an important influence on library practice in other countries in the region—probably third in importance after the United States and Britain.

Australia was the first country in the region to adopt the Dewey Decimal Classification widely. In the 1890s, the period immediately prior to Federation, public and academic libraries started to adopt the DDC and exchange information about the DDC through the short-lived Library Association of Australasia. Papers explaining the DDC were read at the Institute's conferences in 1898 and 1900.

Before Federation in 1901, libraries that had adopted the DDC in Australia included:

Newcastle School of Arts
Public Lending Library of Victoria
Public Library of South Australia
University of Adelaide
University of Sydney

These were closely followed by the Public Library of New South Wales in 1901.

Between then and the present, the DDC has been the predominant classification in Australia. The first challenge came with a move to Bliss at the Australian National University (ANU) and the University of Tasmania around 1950. Then there was a move (following the trend in the United States) to the Library of Congress Classification. Macquarie University and Canberra CAE (which became the University of Canberra) were established with LCC (in 1965 and 1968, respectively). The Australian National University and the Universities of Queensland and Tasmania converted to LCC around 1970—in the cases of ANU and Tasmania from collections which at the time were a mixture of Bliss and the DDC.

Now, Australian libraries using the DDC include:

- The National Library
- All six state libraries
- Practically all public libraries
- Practically all school libraries
- About 75 percent of academic libraries—with the rest using LCC, and with many law libraries using the Moys classification
- Some special libraries—with the most common classification being the UDC

I suspect that this means that the proportion of libraries using the DDC in Australia is greater than that in any other country.

However, this wide acceptance of the DDC in Australia has not been uncritical. Even the earliest advocates of the DDC were unhappy with the arrangement of "990 Oceanica   Polar Regions" (as it was then called). In 1938, work started on an expansion of the historical periods under 994 Australia, and of the geographic areas within Australia, first by a committee of the Australian Institute of Librarians (AIL), and later by the National Library. The AIL's work on the historical periods was incorporated into the fourteenth edition of the DDC in 1942, while work on the expansion of geographic areas resulted in the publication (in 1971 by the National Library of Australia) of *Australia: DDC Expansion*, and later in the incorporation of the expansion into Edition 20 of the DDC in 1989.

The treatment of Australian literature has been another concern— since it was seen as being distinct from English literature in the same way as American literature. Australian concerns here were resolved in Edition 17 of the DDC, with the provision of options for national literatures like Australian literature.

However, Australians have not only been critical about the classification of material related directly to their country. Class 510 Mathematics has been criticised, with revisions developed in 1966 and 1974 by a group of mathematicians at the University of Sydney who found the DDC unsatisfactory both before and after the phoenix schedule of 510 Mathematics in Edition 18. Another phoenix schedule in that edition, 340 Law, has also been found wanting in Australia, since many academic libraries that use the DDC for the rest of their collections use the Moys classification for law.

There was early influence on the Classification through correspondence between H.C.L. Anderson (of the Public Library of New South Wales) and Melvil Dewey in the 1890s and 1900s. Formal mechanisms for Australian input have been set up four times:

- In 1938–1942, with the Committee on the Cataloguing of Australiana of the Australian Institute of Librarians;

- In 1966–1967, with the Committee on Dewey Decimal Classification of the Australian Advisory Council on Bibliographical Services;

- In 1974–1985, with the Decimal Classification Liaison Committee of the Library Association of Australia; and

- In 1993–1996, with the appointment by OCLC Forest Press of an Australian representative from the Australian Committee on Cataloguing (ACOC) to the Decimal Classification Editorial Policy Committee (EPC).

Thus, as well as using the Dewey Decimal Classification widely, Australian libraries have had a long history of influencing the development of the Classification.

NEW ZEALAND AND THE PACIFIC

I have not been able to find out when Dewey was first used in New Zealand, but it cannot have been very long after its adoption in Australia. Certainly, by the time of the Munn-Barr report in 1934,[1] the Dewey Decimal Classification was being used in all larger libraries. This predominance continued until the 1970s, when there was a strong move among academic libraries in New Zealand to the LC Classification. The situation now is that the DDC is used by the National Library of New Zealand, all public and school libraries, and most libraries in the polytechnics and colleges of education. Five of the university libraries use the LC Classification, and the other two use Dewey. One significant recent development in New Zealand has been the National Library's expansion of the area table —93 New Zealand.

Papua New Guinea uses the DDC in almost all libraries, probably because of the strong Australian influence there.

The island nations of the Pacific often follow the United States pattern—the DDC in public and school libraries, and LCC in academic libraries.

SOUTHEAST ASIA

While earlier cultural influences on Southeast Asia have come from the neighbouring civilisations of China and India, more recent influences have been from Occidental civilisation. In particular, libraries have been strongly influenced by librarians from the United States, Britain, and Australia. This means that in library classification, the DDC and LC Classification systems have become widely used, with some revision of the DDC to meet local needs.

The earliest libraries in Southeast Asia to use Dewey may have been school libraries in the Philippines, which changed from the LC Classification to the DDC in 1919. Since then, the general pattern in the region has been that public libraries and school libraries use

Dewey, while academic libraries are divided between the Dewey Decimal Classification and the LC Classification.

EAST ASIA

While Western influences on library practice have been strong in East Asia, local needs in China, Japan, and Korea have resulted in local classification schemes being developed. These are often based on the DDC decimal notation, but use fundamentally different classes. The local schemes include Lai's scheme which is widely used in Taiwan, the Nippon Decimal Classification in Japan, and the Korean Decimal Classification in South Korea. In addition, a number of schemes have been developed in China, earlier ones based on a traditional view of knowledge, and later ones based on a Marxist-Leninist view. However, I'll leave a more detailed look at practice in China to the next speaker, Wang Dongbo.

Some libraries in East Asia class material in Chinese, Japanese, or Korean one way, and Western-language material another way. For example, the commonest pattern for libraries in Taiwan is to use Lai's New Classification for Chinese libraries for Chinese-language material, and the DDC for Western-language material. In academic libraries in Hong Kong, the second commonest pattern is to use the DDC for English-language material and the Lai scheme for Chinese (in case you're wondering, the commonest is the LC Classification for all material).

SOUTH ASIA

The first library to use the DDC in South Asia was probably the Punjab University Library in 1914—a library in British India, where an American, A.D. Dickinson, was university librarian. Ten years later in 1924, S.R. Ranganathan started to develop his Colon Classification, convinced of the inadequacy of the DDC and of other currently used schemes: Cutter's Expansive Classification, the LC Classification, and James Duff Brown's Subject Classification. Although the Colon Classification has not replaced the DDC as the most widely used classification scheme in South Asia, the intellectual foundations of Ranganathan's scheme have influenced the later development of the DDC—not in the decimal notation, but in the more rigorous analysis of subjects and in the greater ability to provide a notation for complex subjects.

Librarians other than Ranganathan have grappled with the inadequacies and cultural biases of the DDC. Over the years, India has probably been the most prolific source of revisions of the DDC, particularly in dealing with problems in the classification of Indological material. Unfortunately, in spite of this work, the DDC remains weak in areas of relevance to South Asia, such as 181.4 Philosophy of India and 294 Religions of Indic origin.

FOR THE FUTURE

The Asia-Pacific region is currently increasing in economic importance, and doubtless libraries will progress in the region as part of this economic development. I believe that the Dewey Decimal Classification should build on its wide use within the region by making greater provision for local needs. This could involve:

- More detailed expansions of parts of Table 2. In Table 2, —73–79 United States is expanded to the level of the more than 3,000 counties, while —51 China and —54 India (both countries with much larger populations) are only divided to the level of the provinces or states. Libraries in the different countries in the region should consider whether more detailed expansion is needed for their parts of Table 2.

- Revisions of the parts of the schedules relating to the philosophies, religions, and other cultural aspects of the region. Classes 296 Judaism and 297 Islam have been revised in Edition 21 of Dewey. Do other parts of the schedules need revision too?

Work on the revision of Table 2 could be done by national libraries or national library associations, in cooperation with the editor of the DDC and with the Editorial Policy Committee, since area tables, by their nature, are confined to a particular country. Other work to revise the schedules would require international cooperation, since cultural phenomena like philosophy and religion cross national boundaries.

Another project for the future might involve a more detailed survey of classification practice in the Asia-Pacific region than the one I have been able to carry out here. The last such survey was completed in 1964 by Pauline A. Seely and Sarah K. Vann. While libraries are slow to change classification schemes, much will have happened since then.

NOTE

1. Ralph Munn and John Barr, *A Survey of Conditions and Suggestions for Their Improvement* (Christchurch, N.Z.: Library Association of New Zealand, 1934).

The Dewey Decimal Classification in China
Wang Dongbo

INTRODUCTION

Starting with a brief history of Chinese classification systems before the DDC was introduced into China, I shall discuss the impact and influence of the DDC upon Chinese librarianship in the past and in the future.[1] In addition, outlines of some influential library classifications are listed.

CHINESE CLASSIFICATION SYSTEMS BEFORE THE DDC WAS INTRODUCED INTO CHINA

China has an age-old tradition of classification systems. In the long history of feudal society, the two predominant classification systems were Qi Fen Fa ("Seven-Division Classification," hereafter referred to as SDC), which originated in Qi Lue in the Han Dynasty, and Si Ku Fa ("Four-Division Classification," the classification for Si Ku Quan Shu, hereafter referred to as FDC), which was used in the Si Ku Quan Shu Zong Mu (General Catalogue of "Si Ku Quan Shu") in the Qing Dynasty. After the Opium War in 1840, Western thought began to be introduced into China, and the sciences in China were divided into Old Sciences and New Sciences. The traditional SDC and FDC could no longer cover the new publications appearing at that time, so new classification systems were developed to accommodate the new disciplines. In 1896, Kang Youwei compiled Xi Xue Shu Mu Biao (A Bibliography of Western Sciences), which consisted of three divisions: Xue (Sciences), Zheng (Politics), and Za (Miscellanies). In the same year, Liang Qichao compiled Riben Shu Mu Zhi (A Japanese Bibliography), which included fifteen classes, such as Politics, Industry, Commerce, etc. In addition, some people modified subdivisions in FDC to suit their own needs.

THE DDC'S IMPACT ON CHINESE CLASSIFICATION SYSTEMS

1. The DDC began to be used in some libraries in China.

As is known, the DDC is one of the first modern library classification systems in the world. Since Sun Yuxiu first introduced it in *Jiao Yu Za Zhi* (*Education Journal*) in 1909, the DDC became known and accepted by Chinese librarians. The DDC was used to organize catalogues and collections in some libraries, especially Christian libraries and Christian college libraries, e.g., Wuchang Wen Hua Gong Shu Lin (Boone Library at Wuchang), St. John's University Library in Shanghai, Yali University (Yale-in-China) Library at Changsha,

Yenching University Library, and Tsing Hua Imperial College Library in Peking. When the People's Republic of China was founded in 1949, some libraries were still using the DDC, among which were eleven large-scale libraries such as Shanghai Transportation University Library, Dalian University Library, and Heilongjiang Provincial Library. For awhile, some libraries still used the DDC for the classification of monographs in Western languages. For example, Peking University Library used the DDC for classifying monographs in Western and Russian languages until 1975 and even used the DDC for classifying Western literature and philosophy until May 1991. Beijing Normal University Library used the DDC until 1966. When Furen University (the Catholic university in Peking) and Peiping Normal University were merged into Beijing Normal University in 1953, Furen was using LCC and PNU was using the DDC. Tsinghua University Library used the DDC until 1964. Northwest University Library (in Xi'an) used the DDC from 1937 until 1993 (the fourteenth, sixteenth, and nineteenth editions were used in the library).

2. Some library classifications were compiled on the basis of the DDC.

Although the DDC is good in most aspects, it was not fully suitable to Chinese libraries since it was compiled mainly for American libraries. There was a need for the modification of the DDC. During the years after the DDC was introduced into China, many Chinese library scientists studied it and compiled some classifications "to complement the DDC," "to imitate the DDC," or "to modify the DDC."

i) "To complement the DDC"

"To complement the DDC" is to compile classification systems by adding some new classes into the DDC to cover ancient Chinese books, such as Duwei Shu Mu Shi Lei Fa Bu Bian (A Supplement to the DDC) by Zha Xiu in 1925 and Zhong Wai Tu Shu Tong Yi Fen Lei Fa (A United Classification for Chinese and Foreign Books) by Wang Yunwu in 1928. As Wang Yunwu put it, "the DDC is suitable to Chinese libraries and should be expanded to cover Chinese books." So, Wang's classification copied the DDC and added three special symbols, +, ++, and ‡, before the original DDC numbers to form new classification numbers and to express concepts not covered in the DDC.

ii) "To imitate the DDC"

"To imitate the DDC" is to compile classification systems by imitating the DDC structure, among which are Fang Duwei Shu Mu Shi Lei Fa (A Classification System Imitating the DDC) by Shen Zurong and Hu Qingsheng and published by Wuchang Wen Hua Gong Shu Lin (Boone Library) in 1917. Its principle is "to create a new classification and to include both Chinese and foreign books." Most classes of this system were translated from the DDC and others were extracted from FDC. Shi Jie Tu Shu Fen Lei Fa (A World Library Classification) by Du Dingyou in 1921 is another one of this kind.

iii) "To modify the DDC"

"To modify the DDC" is to change some classes in the DDC to accommodate Chinese books. Zhongguo Tu Shu Shi Jin Fen Lei Fa (Decimal Classification for Chinese Books) compiled by He Rizhang and Yuan Yongjin in 1934, and Zhongguo Shi Jin Fen Lei Fa (Chinese Decimal Classification) compiled by Pi Gaopin are examples of this kind of modification. Although their subdivisions are different from those in the DDC, their structure and dividing principles are similar to the DDC.

In addition, there are some classification systems adopting only DDC principles and not DDC structure, e.g., Zhongguo Tu Shu Fen Lei Fa (Classification Scheme for Chinese Books) compiled by Liu Guojun in 1929 and Harvard-Yenching Chinese Books Classification by Qiu Kaiming in 1932. The two classification systems developed in the early period of the People's Republic of China that also adopted only DDC principles and not DDC structure are Dong Bei Tu Shu Guan Tu Shu Fen Lei Fa (Classification for Northeast Library) in 1948 and Tu Shu Fen Lei Xin Fa (A New Library Classification) by Shandong Provincial Library in 1949.

These classifications have had some influence in Chinese librarianship and have found some applications. For example, the Chinese Decimal Classification was used in Peking University Library and Wuhan University Library, the Decimal Classification for Chinese Books in Beijing Normal University Library, the World Library Classification in Sun Yatsen University Library and Suzhou Library, and the United Classification for Chinese and Foreign Books in Zhejiang Provincial Library. The Classification Scheme for Chinese Books used in Nanking University Library and the National Library of China became a blueprint of Zhongguo Tu Shu Fen Lei Fa (New Classification Scheme for Chinese Libraries) that was compiled by Lai Yongxiang and has been used by most libraries in Taiwan Province ever since.

The introduction of the DDC solved the problem of classification for new publications at that time and promoted the emergence and development of modern Chinese classification systems. The classification systems of this period began to be independent of bibliographies; they became real classification systems, with scientific notation systems and practical compilation techniques. Thus, decimal systems completely replaced FDC and SDC.

THE DDC'S INFLUENCE ON CONTEMPORARY CHINESE LIBRARIANSHIP

The Chinese government has been putting emphasis on the compilation and use of library classification since the foundation of Socialist China in 1949 and has authorized the compilation of some large-scale comprehensive classification systems, such as Zhongguo Tu Shu Guan Tu Shu Fen Lei Fa in 1973 (Chinese Library Classification, hereafter referred to as CLC) and Zhongguo Ke Xue Yuan Tu Shu Guan Fen Lei Fa in 1958 (Classification for Libraries of the Chinese Academy of Sciences). Thus, Chinese libraries began to use common classification systems. Those libraries that used the DDC or other classifications based on the DDC turned to CLC and other new classifications compiled after 1949. Therefore, the DDC as such ceased to be used in China.

As I mentioned above, the DDC once had a great influence on Chinese librarianship. Its influence still exists now, although the DDC or other classifications based on the DDC are no longer in use.

1. Studies, research, and translations

Chinese classification researchers and librarians are still studying the DDC as one of the authoritative classifications in the world.

Firstly, many Chinese universities teach the DDC in their "Classification and Cataloguing" or other courses. The Departments of Library and Information Science in Peking University and Wuhan University have the subject "DDC Studies" for graduate students, and there are always several dissertations or research articles on the DDC every year. There is an entry on the DDC in the Library and Information Science Section, Great Chinese Encyclopedia. Pi Gaopin, a professor at Wuhan University, published several articles on the DDC: "DC Jian Jie Yu Ping Pan (A Critical Introduction to the DDC)" appeared in 1979 (32 pages); "Ping Di 19 Ban DC (A Review of the Nineteenth Edition of the DDC)" appeared in 1985 (35 pages); and "Ping Di 20 Ban De DC (A Review of the Twentieth Edition of the DDC)" appeared in 1992 (40 pages). Other articles mainly focus on comparative studies between the DDC and Chinese classifications, especially CLC, such as comparisons of class annotations, standard subdivisions, compilation techniques, etc.

Secondly, the DDC is still used as a reference tool in the revision of currently existing classification systems. We borrow some methods of the DDC in the processing of new disciplines or subjects. In new editions, we still follow the DDC technique of not immediately reusing numbers that have recently been vacated.

Thirdly, the editorial board of CLC once tried to translate the DDC nineteenth edition and the DDC twentieth edition into Chinese, but failed for various reasons. We are now applying to OCLC for translation rights to the twenty-first edition of the DDC, so as to promote the influence of the DDC in China and the study of library classification in China.

2. The DDC as a reference tool in cataloguing

The DDC is still an important reference tool in the classification of monographs in Western languages. Most books published in Western countries have DDC numbers in their CIP data. Although few libraries in China are using the DDC to process monographs in Western languages, the library cataloguer can still use DDC numbers in CIP to determine the subjects of books they catalogue and then use CLC to get the correct class numbers.

3. Use of the DDC

In the information age, Chinese libraries are considering sharing their bibliographic data with libraries all around the world. It seems necessary to attach some commonly used classification numbers to Chinese bibliographical data, among which DDC numbers would be one of the best choices. We are considering not only the translation of the DDC (if a license to translate is granted), but also the compilation of a cross-reference index of the DDC and CLC.

CONCLUSIONS AND RECOMMENDATIONS

The DDC is one of the most influential library classification systems in the world. It once had a great influence upon modern classification systems in China and a certain influence upon contemporary Chinese classifications. Chinese classification researchers and cataloguing librarians are keen to remain aware of the future directions of the DDC and have also been making a great effort to promote the study of the DDC. The DDC was once used directly in some libraries in China. It is now used as a reference tool for the cataloguing of monographs in Western languages and for the revision of Chinese library classification systems. It will probably be used in the future as one of the classification numbers in the data of the *Chinese National Bibliography*. Finally, the author would like to make a recommendation that the DDC should consider its responsibility as an international universal classification system by making an effort to eliminate excessive Americanisms in the DDC, by adopting good experiences in other classification systems, and by supporting the translation of the DDC into foreign languages even more than it does now.

NOTE

1. The following background sources were consulted in the preparation of this paper: Li Xiaoyuan, "Zhongguo tu shu guan shi ye guo qu shi nian zhi fa zhan" (Progress of Chinese Librarianship during the Past Ten Years), *Tu shu guan xue ji kan (Library Science Quarterly)*, 10, no. 4 (1936): 507–50; Liu Guojun, "Zhongguo tu shu fen lei fa de fa zhan" (Development of Chinese Classification Systems), *Tu shu guan xue tong xun (Bulletin of China Society for Library Science)*, no. 2 (1981): 46–59; Lu Zhongyue, "Jin dai xi fang Duwei shi jin fen lei fa de chuan ru ji qi ying xiang" (The Introduction and Influences of Dewey in China), *Gui tu xue kan (Guizhou Library Journal)*, no. 2 (1983): 24–29; Shi Lijun, "Duwei fa dui wo guo jin dai tu shu fen lei fa xing cheng he fa zhan de zhong yao zuo yong" (The Important Role of Dewey in the Formation and Development of Chinese Library Classification Systems), *Shandong tu shu guan ji kan (Shandong Library Quarterly)*, no. 3 (1991): 31–36.

APPENDIX

Outlines of Some Influential Library Classifications

I. Decimal Classification for Chinese Books by He Rizhang and Yuan Yongjin in 1934

000 Generalities
100 Philosophy
200 Religion
300 Social Sciences
400 Language and Writing Systems
500 Natural Sciences
600 Applied Sciences
700 Arts
800 Literature
900 History and Geography

II. Chinese Decimal Classification by Pi Gaopin in 1934

000 Generalities
100 Philosophy
200 Religion
300 Social Sciences
400 Language and Writing Systems
500 Natural Sciences
600 Industry and Technology
700 Arts
800 Literature
900 History (including History and Biography, Geography, Archaeology)

III. Classification Scheme for Chinese Books by Liu Guojun in 1929

000 Generalities
100 Philosophy
200 Religion
300 Natural Sciences
400 Applied Sciences
500 Social Sciences
600/700 History and Geography
800 Language and Literature
900 Arts

IV. World Library Classification by Du Dingyou in 1922

000 Generalities
100 Philosophic Science
200 Educational Science
300 Social Sciences
400 Arts
500 Natural Sciences
600 Applied Sciences
700 Language and Writing Systems
800 Literature
900 History and Geography

V. Classification imitating Dewey Decimal Classification by Shen Zurong and Hu Qingsheng in 1917

000 Classics and Encyclopaedia
100 Philosophy and Religion
200 Sociology and Education
300 Politics and Economics
400 Medicine
500 Sciences
600 Applied Sciences
700 Arts
800 Literature
900 History

VI. United Classification for Chinese and Foreign Books by Wang Yunwu in 1928

000 Generalities
100 Philosophy
200 Religion
300 Social Sciences
400 Language
500 Natural Sciences
600 Applied Sciences
700 Arts
800 Literature
900 History and Geography

VII. Classification for Northeast Library by Northeast Library in 1948

0   Generalities
1   Philosophy
2   Religion
3   Social Sciences
4   Natural Sciences
5   Applied Technology
6   Language and Philology
7   Literature
8   Arts
9   History and Geography

VIII. New Library Classification by Shandong Provincial Library in 1949

100   Generalities
200   Philosophy
300   Education
400   Social Sciences
500   Language and Philology
600   Natural Sciences
700   Applied Technology
800   Arts
900   History and Geography

IX. Chinese Library Classification by CLC Editorial Board in 1973

A   Marxism-Leninism and Mao Zedong Thought
B   Philosophy
C   Social Sciences in General
D   Politics and Laws
E   Military Affairs
F   Economics
G   Culture, Sciences, Education and Sports
H   Languages and Writing Systems
I   Literature
J   Arts
K   History and Geography
N   Natural Sciences in General
O   Physico-mathematical Sciences and Chemistry
P   Astronomy and Geoscience
Q   Biological Science
R   Medicine and Hygiene
S   Science of Agriculture

T	Industry and Technology
U	Communication and Transportation
V	Aeronautics and Astronautics
X	Environmental Science and Safety Science
Z	Comprehensive works

X.   Classification for Library of Chinese Science Academy by CLCSA Editorial Board in 1958

00	Marxism-Leninism and Mao Zedong Thought
10	Philosophy
20	Social Sciences (General)
21	History and Historical Science
27	Economy and Economics
31	Political Affairs and Social Lives
34	Law and Science of Law
36	Military Affairs and Military Science
37	Culture, Sciences, Education and Sports
41	Language and Philology
42	Literature
48	Arts
49	Atheism and Religion
50	Natural Sciences (General)
51	Mathematics
52	Mechanics
53	Physics
54	Chemistry
55	Astronomy
56	Geoscience
58	Biology
61	Medicine and Hygiene
65	Science of Agriculture
71	Engineering and Technology
90	Comprehensive works

Translating the DDC:
The Experience of the
Spanish Version
Octavio G. Rojas L.

INTRODUCTION

When we first began discussing with Peter Paulson, executive director of OCLC Forest Press, the possibility of translating into Spanish the twentieth edition of the Dewey Decimal Classification, and even during the initial contact we had with the late John A. Humphry, we knew that the project would be a complex and hard task. The reality was that the project exceeded all expectations and was much more complex and difficult than we had anticipated. This not only made it more interesting for those who participated in its development, but also made it an extraordinary challenge, especially due to the time frame initially foreseen for its development: eight to ten months.

Once we agreed with Peter Paulson on the basic terms of the project, Rojas Eberhard Editores was able to convince Information Handling Services (a company located in Denver, Colorado, known worldwide for its products and services in the field of technological information) to participate with us in this translation and publication project. Information Handling Services channeled its participation through its subsidiary in Mexico, to facilitate the integration of the project into the main zone of influence of the final product: Latin America.

Once the final terms of the project were agreed upon among OCLC Forest Press, Information Handling Services, and Rojas Eberhard Editores, a team was formed at Rojas Eberhard Editores under the general direction of the undersigned, and under the technical direction of Margarita Amaya de Heredia, a well-known Colombian professional with wide experience in the field of technical processes, who, fortunately for the project, had just been pensioned by the Department of Libraries of the National University of Colombia. At the same time, the translators were selected, by subject specialty, from a list of experts and professional librarians of recognized experience. An International Advisory Committee was established, including among its members Miriam Pirela, who is responsible for the management of the authority files in the Autonomous Institute of the National Library of Venezuela and a professor of classification in the School of Libraries and Records Management of the Universidad Central in Caracas; Bertha Nelly Cardona de Gil, Director of the Inter-American School of Library

Sciences of the University of Antioquia, well known for her participation in the direction of the project of Listas de Encabezamientos de Materia para Bibliotecas (LEMB) of ICFES (Colombia) and the OAS; and Ageo Garcia, Head of Classification of the Academic Information Center of the Ibero American University of Mexico, D.F., who lived in Austin, Texas, where he received a Master's degree in Information Science and worked on classification and cataloging projects.

At the same time, a coordination plan was agreed upon with the Dewey Editorial Office in the Decimal Classification Division of the Library of Congress of the United States, the unit responsible for the development of the Dewey system, with the advice of an Editorial Policy Committee, whose members are mentioned in the preface of the original edition in English. The Division operates as part of an agreement between the Library of Congress and OCLC Forest Press, owner of the DDC copyright. The coordination of our project was made through Joan Mitchell, the editor of the DDC and a member of OCLC Forest Press. The project had the strong support and advice of the Division staff, through long sessions in the offices of the Division at the Library of Congress and through communications by fax and telephone.

SCOPE OF THE TRANSLATION

As a fundamental starting point, it was decided that, because of time constraints, the project should be a translation, not an adaptation, of DDC 20. This was decided despite the interest of Spanish users in adaptations of such subjects as religion, law, literature, history, and geography (schedules and tables). To solve this problem, it was decided it would be more practical to publish later supplements for one or more of these topics. In this way, we would be able to develop these adaptations carefully, taking full advantage of the advances in the twenty-first edition of the DDC.

This decision was also heavily influenced by the fact that the twentieth English edition was published six years ago (in 1979), while the last Spanish edition, which is dated 1980, is in actuality based on the eighteenth edition in English, which was published in 1971. These facts make the 1980 Spanish edition an obsolete working tool for the development of libraries in Latin America.

In spite of the decision to translate, not adapt DDC 20, some minor but necessary adjustments were made based on DDC 21, in particular in the areas of history and geography (Table 2). We believed it would

78

have been a disservice to libraries in Latin America to publish a work that ignored the recent changes in Eastern Europe or the adjustments for Latin America that had already been incorporated into Edition 21. On the other hand, due to the basic agreement, the developments in Table 2 in the 1980 Spanish edition, which are quite detailed, were not included; they would have required careful and expensive research to be updated. As a special concession, however, the geographic numbers of regions taken from that edition have been included in the Relative Index.

The three tables that have been updated based on the twenty-first English edition are:

Table 2
—47 Eastern Europe　　Russia

—49 Other parts of Europe
—4957 Eastern Macedonia and the Thrace region
—4958 Former Aegean Sea Islands region

—497 Yugoslavia, Croatia, Slovenia, Bosnia and Hercegovina, Macedonia
—498 Romania
—499 Bulgaria (*formerly* —4977)

—72 Mesoamerica (Middle America)

Middle America is the name for the region that extends from Mexico to Panama, and includes the West Indies and Bermuda (called Mesoamerica in the last Spanish edition). Mesoamerica is the name of the cultural region where the Aztec and Mayan high civilizations were developed, and is located in the geographic region covered by Middle America (Middle America of DDC 20).

Table 5
—97 North American native peoples
—98 South American native peoples

Table 6
—97 North American native languages
—98 South American native languages

For the native languages of North and South America, it was possible to widen the spectrum of these languages to include Huasteco and Mame (—97415), Huichol, Tarahumara, and Yaquí (—9745), Chinanteco and Otomí (—976), Matagalpa and Paya (—978), Cayapa, Coconuco, and Paéz (—982), Cocama (—9838), and Cayapó (—984), thanks to the participation of Ageo Garcia, member of the International Advisory Committee, and to the collaboration and supervision of Julianne Beall, assistant editor, DDC.

The schedules of the twenty-first edition were used in the following parallel cases:

Schedule 400
497 North American native languages
498 South American native languages

Schedule 800
897 Literatures of North American native languages
898 Literatures of South American native languages

Schedule 900
947 Eastern Europe   Russia
949.58 Former Aegean Islands region
949.59 Crete region
949.7 Yugoslavia, Croatia, Slovenia, Bosnia and Hercegovina, Macedonia
949.8 Romania
949.9 Bulgaria [*formerly* 949.77]

The schedules of the twenty-first edition were also used for all countries of South America. The schedule for Colombian history was reviewed and updated. In Table 2, some adjustments were made to Colombia, but due to technical reasons and the tight timetable for publication, it was not possible to make all the changes that the editors of the Spanish edition would have wanted. The option was left open for a future special supplement for Latin America.

DECISIONS BASED ON USER CONVENIENCE

In schedules 560, 580, and 590, the biologists that collaborated in the translation considered convenience for users in the decision to maintain the Greek or Latin form of the scientific names of plants and animals, as they appear in DDC 20. For schedules 560 Paleontology and paleozoology, 580 Botanical sciences, and 590 Zoological sciences, the following was determined: the headings of the main summaries of each of these schedules were included in the Spanish form because they are well-known terms, while the names corresponding to species, genuses, and families of plants and animals (low taxons) were kept in their Greek and Latin form, as they appear in DDC 20.

For practical reasons, the following sections of DDC 20 in English were not included: the Relocations and Reductions Tables, the

Comparative Tables for Music and for British Columbia, and the Equivalence Tables for Music and for British Columbia. These tables make reference to comparisons between the nineteenth and twentieth English editions. Since the majority of the Spanish-speaking users in Latin America are not familiar with Edition 19, either because they do not speak English or have never purchased Edition 19, a comparison between Editions 19 and 20 could lead to confusion. Nevertheless, in the schedules there are notes about the changes and relocations in order to help users assess number allocation. The classifier who has been working with Spanish Edition 18 must analyze the changes with caution and make the decisions that are most suitable for his or her particular case.

STYLE PROBLEMS

Although a great effort was made to avoid direct textual translation, the structure of this kind of work always creates limitations for free interpretations or idiomatic adaptations. In this regard, everything possible was done to avoid the use of the passive voice, which is so common in English, and to keep short sentences without too many adornments, considering that this work is a consultation tool and not a literary text.

Since the work was translated and edited mainly by Colombian personnel, a special effort was made to avoid Colombianisms in the work so that it could offer clear terminology for all Spanish-speaking countries. For this purpose, we used the last edition of the *Colombian Language Academy Dictionary* as a final arbitrator in the majority of cases, and we also had the collaboration of the foreign members of the International Advisory Committee. Obviously, given the complex nature of the developments, as well as regional and national neologisms, it was very difficult to produce a work whose terminology is clear for 100 percent of its users.

In the case of English terms that do not yet have an equivalent translation in Spanish, it was necessary to go more to the definition than to the translation; this happened in the computer area, which includes words such as "software" and "firmware." Where these kinds of words were found, we had two alternatives: leave the word in English or use the closest translation, based on our criteria, leaving the word in English in brackets. We thought that with this method the user would have a clearer idea of the text reference and intention. In addition, the words used in foreign languages are highlighted in italics. Diacritical signs were included for the following languages: Spanish, French, Italian, and Portuguese.

It is necessary to mention here that with regard to English names, it was decided as a basic policy not to translate proper names into Spanish. However, as an exception, those names that are of common use were translated, for example, New York, London, and North Carolina. Regarding geographic features, only the feature was translated; for example, Black River was translated as "Rio Black."

Since the translation was made collectively, that is, by distributing sections among several people in accordance with their specialty, experience, and knowledge of the Dewey system, the revision and integration process to give the work the unity required was exceedingly difficult, although the contribution of each translator was respected as much as possible. We hope that we have achieved the coherence and integrity we were seeking. Information Handling Services and Rojas Eberhard Editores, as sponsors of this translation, beyond the risks and commercial opportunities, desired mainly to render a service to the community of Spanish-speaking librarians in particular, and to the library development of the Latin American region in general. There is no doubt that an updated version of the work was required and, obviously, in the region's own language.

As has been said in previous English and Spanish editions, it is absolutely impossible to produce a perfect work, given the dynamic itself of the different interpretations that may be given to any scheme aiming to classify the full range of human knowledge. In this new Spanish edition, we tried as much as possible to maintain the professional seriousness and rigorousness of the previous editions in Spanish and the English originals. There is no doubt that the work is not finished yet. We hope it will be used by classifiers and general users who will improve and enrich it through their analysis and comments. They should send their suggestions to the Decimal Classification Division of the Library of Congress, where, we are sure, they will always be welcome. We hope to give continuity to the revisions through supplements aimed at a future Spanish edition.

IMPORTANT CONSIDERATIONS IN A TRANSLATION PROJECT

In hindsight we have some suggestions for future Dewey translators:

1. We think the first decision that should be made at the start of a project as complex as this is the selection of the technical coordinator, who has to be full-time, and the selection of the translators, who should not only be bilingual, but also should have the

time necessary to do the terminology research and confirmation inherent in translation work.

2. The next decision has to deal with the selection of publishing software. We selected PageMaker, which is very well known in our country, but we could not use its utility to build the index, since the DDC Relative Index is unique and different from common book indexes. To work with the index, we built a database using CDS/ISIS, the UNESCO software, converted it to a text file and then to PageMaker, where we edited it.

3. Finally, we believe that the most difficult part of the project was the preparation of the Relative Index. The index has to be done after the schedules have been completed, in order to have consistency in the use of terminology. Every entry has to be checked carefully and this is very time-consuming.

We believe this has been a very worthwhile and useful project. We learned a great deal about the pitfalls inherent in such a major translation undertaking, and are now more aware of ways to circumvent these pitfalls. In the meantime, we hope librarians in the Spanish-speaking community worldwide will find this new translation a helpful and up-to-date tool for the organization of their collections.

Dewey Decimal Classification
Organizing the World of Knowledge
for the World

SUMMARY AND CLOSING REMARKS
Lois Mai Chan

INTRODUCTION

In respect to the nature and quantity of available information, 1876 was a very different world from the one we know in the 1990s. Yet in spite of over a century of changes, the Dewey Decimal Classification (DDC), the system that helped organize a small college library, has grown to one that is helping the whole world organize its vast store of information resources. In this closing session, I would like to summarize some of the major factors that have contributed so far to the Dewey system's success as an information organization tool. I will also discuss ongoing efforts to ensure its viability in the future.

MAJOR CHARACTERISTICS OF THE DDC

Structure

The DDC is a universal scheme that maps the universe of knowledge into a hierarchy from the broadest subjects to very narrow topics. Each of the ten *main classes* is divided into ten *divisions*, and each division into ten *sections*, with further subdivisions as required. Because each level is subordinate to the level above it, a simple and logical hierarchical system is formed that progresses from the general to the specific.

Some may feel that a two-dimensional hierarchy is inadequate for handling some of the complex subjects of the modern world. Complex polyhierarchical structures have great theoretical and aesthetic appeal, but they are often very difficult to use consistently. Between the intellectual appeal of a complex polyhierarchical structure and the practicality of a simple one with sufficient details to deal with most subjects, the DDC has chosen the latter. (The Relative Index, it is worth noting here, goes some way toward eliminating any shortcomings in a simple hierarchy.) In this matter, I believe that the fact that the DDC's simple and logical structure is easy to comprehend and manipulate accounts to a large extent for the scheme's enduring popularity.

Notation

To denote the subjects in his scheme, Dewey decided to use simple Arabic numerals, with the symbols 0 through 9 treated like decimal fractions. A decimal notation enables infinite expansion and subdivision without disturbing other topics already classed. Furthermore, Arabic numerals transcend language barriers, and their self-evident numerical sequence facilitates ordering, whether on shelves or in printed or electronically displayed lists. The use of a single punctuation mark, the dot, keeps the notation simple and makes it clear how the classes are ordered.

The DDC notation reflects the hierarchical order of the Classification, showing the relationship between each level of knowledge and its superordinate and subordinate elements. Dewey's immediate purpose in using decimal notation was to reveal the coordination and subordination of subjects. Though notation cannot reveal the importance or value of a subject, it can display the subject's relative status and location among other subjects in the universe of knowledge. Notation can also show the relative breadth or depth of a subject and its relation to the subjects to its left and right on the shelf. Furthermore, this characteristic particularly facilitates online searching. The searcher can broaden or narrow a search by reducing or adding a digit to the class number.

In this way, the notation reveals the Classification conceptually and visibly. What Dewey did not foresee was that its hierarchical notation has made his scheme highly amenable to machine manipulation, enhancing its usefulness in the machine environment.

Over the years, for various reasons—not the least of which is the desire to have shorter numbers—irregularity in hierarchy has crept into the system. In recent years, the editors have made conscientious efforts to regularize. Many examples of regularization in Edition 21 were shown in today's workshop.

Mnemonics

In assigning numbers to subjects, Dewey frequently used consistent numbers for recurring subjects, a practice that has been retained through subsequent editions. This device helps readers to recognize and remember class numbers more easily. In the earlier editions, consistent numbering was used most prominently for form and geographical divisions, and for languages and literature; gradually, use of the device has become standard practice for several other aspects of the system. Consistent numbering has been a help to classifiers and to searchers. Furthermore, it has enabled the transformation of the scheme from a basically enumerative system to one that is more analytico-synthetic because many elements in class numbers can be readily isolated and identified.

Faceting and synthesis

In an important way, standard subdivisions and mnemonics foreshadowed modern theories of and approaches to organizing information—faceting and synthesis. As A. C. Foskett has pointed out, even in the earlier editions of the DDC, "a very clear facet structure" is discernible in some places, notably Class 400 Philology. Although, he goes on to say, "Dewey does not appear to have seen the real significance of this, and it was left to Ranganathan some fifty years later to make explicit and generalize the principle which is implicit and restricted in this example; nevertheless, in this as in many other points, Dewey showed the way ahead at a very early stage."[1]

In response to the need to handle increasingly complex subjects, the DDC editors of recent editions have turned more and more toward faceting. The trend has been particularly evident since Edition 18, when several more auxiliary tables were included. The addition of these tables and many more add notes paved the way to a more faceted system—a necessary step for enhancing the DDC's ability to handle multi-aspect subjects. With more rigorously defined categories, Edition 21 is even more faceted than earlier editions.

In its present form, therefore, it can be said that the DDC falls between the two extremes of enumerative and analytico-synthetic classification: it is a semi-analytico-synthetic system. The DDC began as a basically enumerative system, in that the numbers for individual subjects, including compound and complex subjects, were enumerated in the scheme. In the second edition, however, the table for form divisions was introduced; also, certain numbers in the scheme were to be divided like certain other numbers, particularly those pertaining to geographic subdivision. Thus, a limited amount of synthesis, or number building, existed from the early editions. With each new edition of the DDC, there have been more provisions for the synthesis of class numbers, with greater use of facets and facet indicators and more clearly defined citation orders.

Needless to say, although the DDC has not remained as simple as it was in the beginning, it is now much better equipped for the close analysis of knowledge and the subsequent classification of quite narrow (or micro) subjects through synthesis, or number building.

FACTORS CONTRIBUTING TO THE SUCCESS OF THE DDC

The popularity of the DDC is considerable. Although when it was first devised in 1876 it was intended for a small college library, it was not long before libraries all over the United States began to adopt the system. International interest developed fairly quickly, and at the present time slightly more than half of the sales of the English-language edition are to international users. Giles S. Martin reported that libraries in Australia began using the DDC as early as the 1890s. And as Wang Dongbo indicated, it was as early as 1909 that the DDC became known in China and was accepted by Chinese librarians.

To date, the scheme has been translated into over thirty languages, either as it stands or as adapted to particular circumstances. The Italian, Spanish, and Turkish translations are the most recent official translations of the full edition, and the first ever Russian translation is now under way. In his paper, Octavio G. Rojas L. recounted the experience of translating the DDC into Spanish.

There are now DDC users on every continent in the world. In addition, there are numerous instances where the scheme has served as a model for similar schemes designed to suit local needs. Such wide use of the system did not come by accident. I believe there are certain factors that have been instrumental in its success. Briefly summarized, they are:

Universality

Its simple but logical structure and its universally recognizable notation make the Dewey Decimal Classification easy to understand and to apply. Both qualities transcend language and cultural barriers.

Elasticity

The DDC is structured in such a way that it can handle macro as well as micro units of information by adjusting the depth of hierarchy. Its decimal notation allows expansion or contraction of the Classification from the broadest to the narrowest, as evidenced in the various levels of development reflected in the full edition, the abridged edition, and the school summaries. Such elasticity makes the system applicable to different types and sizes of libraries, from the largest, such as the British Library and the National Library of Australia, to the smallest school and village libraries.

Versatility

The Dewey Decimal Classification began as a system for the purpose of classifying books in a library. It has evolved into a system capable of handling many different types of materials—books, serials, nonprint materials, national bibliographies in various formats, and now electronic information. It is equally adaptable to materials on all subjects in all languages in every kind of information environment. John P. Comaromi, the late editor of the DDC, called the DDC the "lingua franca" of librarians.[2] Barbara L. Bell mentioned versatility as one of the strengths of the DDC and cited the way the system can organize information as the reason for using it in a national bibliography. Another example of the DDC's versatility is as an Internet browser. Developed recently by Diane Vizine-Goetz of OCLC, and tailored to the contents of OCLC's NetFirst (a directory of Internet resources), this Internet browser is based on an end-user version of the DDC summaries.[3]

Adaptability

The universal structural principles, notation, elasticity, and versatility of the DDC render the system particularly amenable to modification and adaptation. It is adaptable in several perspectives: spatial, temporal, and cultural. Spatially, information professionals all over the world have found the DDC useful as is or as a model. Wang Dongbo discussed various attempts throughout the history of Chinese libraries to adapt the DDC structure to national needs; as a result there exist many Chinese complements, imitations, and modifications of the DDC itself. Giles Martin and Barbara Bell discussed various existing configurations of the DDC in Africa, Asia, and the Pacific regions. Temporally, the DDC has moved from the latter part of the nineteenth century almost to the end of the twentieth century and into the electronic age, retaining its vigor and vitality throughout. It now seems ready to be just as successful in meeting the challenges of the twenty-first century. Culturally, the DDC has proven to be adaptable to environments with vastly different linguistic and philosophical backgrounds. It is, of course, acknowledged that no system can aspire to be all things to all people; our speakers have commented on areas where the DDC falls short in meeting specific needs. While there are still problems to be solved, areas that need early attention, there is nonetheless reason to expect that the DDC's overall structure and notation will prove to be as adaptable to future circumstances as they have been in the past.

EFFORTS TO KEEP THE DDC VIABLE

The DDC has proven to be a major tool for organizing information throughout the twentieth century. Maintaining its usefulness into the twenty-first century requires constant vigilance and sustained effort. In recent years, such efforts have included accelerated revision and internationalization.

Revision

To remain viable, a subject access system must keep pace with new knowledge; nothing is more important. Continuous, cyclical revision ensures its viability in the rapidly changing information environment. To ensure its currency, the DDC is revised continuously: new editions appear at intervals of seven to ten years, and changes made between editions are published in *Dewey Decimal Classification, Additions, Notes and Decisions (DC&)*. Furthermore, at its headquarters, enormous amounts of energy and resources are devoted to its maintenance and continuing development as an international, not just a national, tool. All those who adopt the system are thus able to benefit from the full range of efforts in revision.

For the DDC, the extent of revision of each discipline in each edition depends primarily on two needs: to accommodate new subjects and to rectify problems. New areas of knowledge, political and social changes, and outdated or biased terminology necessitate reworking of existing classes. When feasible, existing political, racial, and gender biases are corrected. And throughout, there is a constant effort to remove American bias in both structure and terminology.

When opportunities for reworking a schedule or a portion of a schedule arise, DDC editors make increasing use of facet indicators and notational synthesis in order to render the system more flexible and adaptable to complex subjects and new information environments. As Joan S. Mitchell pointed out, in recent years there has been a conscious effort to move the DDC away from an enumerative system to an analytico-synthetic one. Making greater use of facet indicators and notational synthesis enhances the DDC's ability to handle increasingly complex subjects and offers greater potential in machine retrieval of information. Throughout the revisions, there is an ever present effort to make number building easier. In Edition 21, these trends are most obvious in the revision of classes 350 and 570. In many cases, recent revisions reflect modern theory and current thinking in classification. An example is the use of retroactive notation in these new schedules and in the complete revision of 780 Music in Edition 20.[4]

Over the years, many concepts represented by standard subdivisions have been placed in schedule numbers or modified in what is called "displaced" standard subdivisions. In recent editions, many of these irregular standard subdivisions have been regularized in order to move the DDC closer to a truly faceted system.

Three methods of revisions are used: complete, extensive, and routine:

Complete revisions

A complete revision is undertaken when the basic structure of a discipline is so out-of-date that: first, it can no longer accommodate current information; or, second, that it is difficult to apply; or, third, that the order of classes is illogical. A complete revision results in proper placement of new topics and often involves changes in citation order and in how classes are divided. In Edition 21, there are two complete revisions: 350–354 Public administration and 570 Life sciences   Biology. Joan Mitchell summarized the major changes in these schedules, and Giles Martin analyzed why complete revisions were needed and provided detailed discussion and examples of the new schedules. Major changes in these revisions include reversed citation orders and reordered classes.

Extensive revisions

An extensive revision retains the main outline of the schedule, reworking some or many of the subdivisions and making expansions for new topics. In Edition 21, 370 Education is an example of an extensive revision. The basic outline remains the same as in previous editions, but many major topics, such as the education of women and religious schools, have been moved to more appropriate locations. Also, terminology in the captions has been updated or revised to reflect current usage and to accommodate international applications.

Routine revisions

Routine revisions are made constantly. Furthermore, for each new DDC edition, the entire range of classes and the index are re-examined, and routine revisions are made throughout the scheme. Such revisions include inserting new subjects, realigning illogically placed subjects, eliminating dual provisions, pruning rarely used classes, and updating and correcting terminology in both schedule captions and the index.

Joan Mitchell outlined several areas of changes in DDC 21. There are many other changes too numerous to cover in a brief discussion.

Continuous revision

In recent years, OCLC Forest Press, the publisher of the DDC, has implemented a policy of continuous revision between editions. Previously, users had to wait for the next edition in order to be able to apply numbers for new topics. Currently, numbers for new topics and revised numbers are published between editions in *Dewey Decimal Classification, Additions, Notes and Decisions* (*DC&*). With this mechanism in place, users are now able to receive new and revised numbers in a more timely fashion.

Internationalization

From the beginning, the Dewey Decimal Classification has shown a strong American bias. This is manifested in several ways: in terminology, in structure, and in emphasis. Many terms in the captions and the index reflect American usage, particularly for topics relating to political, social, religious, and educational subjects. In structure, the ordering of subjects often represents American thinking or practice. In emphasis, especially in classes such as religion and literature, a greater proportion of the notation has been allotted to U.S.-related topics. For much of the history of the DDC, because of a reluctance to disrupt existing collections, such bias could only be removed gradually, particularly when it was imbedded in the structure. In recent editions, however, much effort has been devoted to rectifying this situation. Edition 21 shows the results of a continuing effort to neutralize terminology in order to remove bias as well as to be more intelligible to international users. When opportunities arise, as in the case of the complete revision of 350–354 Public administration, all structural bias is eliminated and the emphasis is equalized. In Edition 21, we also see the initiation of the multi-edition plan to further reduce Christian bias in 200 Religion.

Other efforts in internationalizing the scheme include enhancement of index terms to provide entry vocabulary for international users and the expansion of many area tables to meet local needs.

Formal mechanisms are now in place to ensure and encourage input from the international community in regard to needed changes. These include international representation on the Decimal Classification Editorial Policy Committee (EPC) and increased communication between the EPC, the editors, and professional library organizations around the world.

Increased ease of application

As the DDC moved through the twentieth century, it became increasingly complex as it attempted to accommodate new knowledge that, in turn, was showing increased complexity. The combination has made the system considerably more difficult to apply. Ever mindful of the needs of classifiers, editors of the recent editions of the DDC have turned their attention to developing various devices to assist them. An indication of such efforts is the proliferation of both the number and the kinds of notes. While notes are always helpful and sometimes essential, the down side is that their increased number and the fine distinctions among different kinds of notes sometimes complicate rather than help their application. In Edition 21, an effort was made to simplify notes.

Since Edition 20, the incorporation of the Manual in the four-volume set is yet another step towards user assistance. As Barbara Bell's survey indicates, users have found the Manual notes helpful for creating DDC numbers and in ensuring consistency in application.

A recent effort to make the scheme more timely and easier to apply is the development of Dewey for Windows. As Julianne Beall mentioned, it is a new product and, as such, still has problems that need to be resolved. As more user feedback is received, these will be worked out. The product shows great promise as a user-friendly tool.

Emphasis on users

The potential of classification as a retrieval tool has become increasingly obvious in the online environment. Joan Mitchell mentioned recent experiments in using DDC summaries to organize World Wide Web sites. Although earlier editions of the DDC were developed and maintained mainly with classifiers in mind, in recent editions, end users' needs are also taken into consideration; the result has been improvements in the index and in the terminology of the captions.

In Julianne Beall's presentation we learned about added index terms in Dewey for Windows, and about other features such as ease in moving up and down the hierarchy, keyword searching, and having both the introduction to the DDC and the glossary online. While Dewey for Windows has been designed specifically to benefit classifiers, it holds great promise as a potential tool for end users.

In sum, in recent years, there has been a substantial effort, much more so than previously, to assist users in applying the DDC.

Training materials are readily available; this workshop itself is another example.

REMAINING CONCERNS AND RECOMMENDATIONS

Users of the DDC, including several speakers at this workshop, have expressed certain concerns relating to the application of the system. Our speakers have also suggested certain improvements; these are summarized below.

Concerns

(1) The need for reclassifying a collection to incorporate relocations and completely revised schedules creates practical problems for libraries using the scheme;

(2) Lack of specificity, particularly in classes relating to language, literature, religion, history, and geography, is a problem for those organizing or developing national bibliographies;

(3) Different definitions of subjects in different contexts create difficulties in application; and

(4) DDC terminology has created considerable difficulty for those who have worked on its translation.

Recommendations

Our speakers have suggested certain improvements, emphasizing, in particular, the following:

(1) Make greater provision for local needs, such as the expansion of Table 2;

(2) Revise the parts of the schedules relating to the philosophies, religions, and other cultural aspects of local regions; and

(3) Continue the removal of existing "Americanisms" in the scheme.

CONCLUSION

The Dewey Decimal Classification is a workable system. The fact that it has survived many storms in the past 120 years and is still the most widely used classification scheme in the world today attests to its practical value.

The decade of the 1990s has been an exciting one for the DDC. Since its acquisition by OCLC, it is being transformed from a basically library-oriented system to a tool capable of organizing information in a variety of environments. Much research is being done on the system. Recent and projected research efforts include developing customized views of the DDC, enhancing links to other thesauri, improving links among DDC editions in different languages, developing a multilingual DDC browser, designing a virtual Dewey library, and using the scheme to categorize Internet resources automatically.

Over the years, there have been many adaptations and modifications of Dewey, which have undoubtedly improved the usefulness of the system for specific localities and clienteles. But in this age of interconnectivity in information access, it is time to consider the benefits of a truly common system. Of course, there is always tension between the need to accommodate local requirements and the need for commonality and compatibility among information providers. The DDC is not yet a perfect system that can be all things to all people, but it keeps pace with new knowledge and is continuously evolving toward universality. Factors mentioned earlier, including its wide adoption to date, indicate that the DDC provides an obvious common ground for meeting the needs of global information flow and exchange. At present, it is a system ready to meet the challenges of the new millennium.

NOTES

1. A. C. Foskett, *The Subject Approach to Information*, 4th ed. (London: Clive Bingley; Hamden, Conn.: Linnet Books, 1982), 316.

2. Lois Mai Chan, John P. Comaromi, Joan S. Mitchell, and Mohinder P. Satija, *Dewey Decimal Classification: A Practical Guide,* 2d ed. (Albany, N.Y.: OCLC Forest Press, 1996), 8.

3. Diane Vizine-Goetz, "Online Classification: Implications for Classifying and Document[-like] Object Retrieval," in *Knowledge Organization and Change: Proceedings of the 4th International ISKO Conference, 15–18 July, Washington, D.C.,* ed. Rebecca Green (Frankfurt/Main: INDEKS Verlag, 1996), 249–53.

4. Retroactive notation occurs when later numbers have precedence over earlier ones. Thus, in number building, one begins with a number coming later in the schedule as the base number, and then adds as instructed from numbers earlier in the sequence.

Contributors

JULIANNE BEALL is Assistant Editor, Dewey Decimal Classification, Decimal Classification Division, Library of Congress. She has held this position since 1986. From 1977 to 1986, Ms. Beall was a Decimal Classification Specialist in the Decimal Classification Division, Library of Congress. Her interests include the electronic use of the DDC, and the international needs of users of the Classification.

BARBARA L. BELL is the Documents/Reference Librarian at The College of Wooster, Wooster, Ohio. She has held this position since 1980. Ms. Bell has done research on national bibliographies from countries around the world and considers the opportunity to work with staff at the National Library of Namibia to create a new national bibliography one of the highlights of her professional life.

LOIS MAI CHAN is Professor of Library and Information Science at the University of Kentucky. She served on the Decimal Classification Editorial Policy Committee for eighteen years, chairing it for six. She has done pioneering work in computer-assisted instruction in the teaching of the DDC, and is the author of many books and articles in the areas of classification and subject analysis.

GILES S. MARTIN is Quality Control Librarian at the University of New South Wales, responsible for authority work and for improving the quality of the University's OPAC. His educational backgound includes a degree in English, work as a Tutor in Mathematics, and a major in Legal Studies. Since 1993 he has been the Australian representative on the Decimal Classification Editorial Policy Committee.

JOAN S. MITCHELL is the Editor of the Dewey Decimal Classification. Ms. Mitchell has been affiliated with the DDC since 1985, when she became a member of the Decimal Classification Editorial Policy Committee, chairing it from 1992 until her appointment as Dewey editor in 1993. She has worked and published in the fields of cataloging and classification, subject access, and the electronic information environment.

WANG DONGBO has held the position of Deputy Director, Department of Chinese Book Cataloguing, National Library of China, since 1995. From 1991–1995, he was Deputy Director, Department of Library Science Research, National Library of China. Mr. Wang has been active in professional organizations both nationally and internationally, including Deputy Director of the Editorial Board of the Chinese Library Classification.

OCTAVIO G. ROJAS L. is the President of Infoenlace Ltda. and Rojas Eberhard Editores, Bogotá, Colombia, organizations that publish and distribute library science materials in Latin America. He was director of the project to translate the twentieth edition of the Dewey Decimal Classification system into Spanish, and is the author of many articles on library development in Colombia and Latin America.

Dewey Decimal Classification: Edition 21 and International Perspectives was designed and composed in Bookman Old Style and Arial typefaces by Lisa Hanifan of Albany, New York. The book was printed and bound by Integrated Book Technology of Troy, New York.